James Ripley Osgood

Companion Poets

Illustrated. Longfellow's Household Poems. Tennyson's Songs for All Seasons.

Browning's Lyrics of Life

James Ripley Osgood

Companion Poets
Illustrated. Longfellow's Household Poems. Tennyson's Songs for All Seasons. Browning's Lyrics of Life

ISBN/EAN: 9783744771733

Printed in Europe, USA, Canada, Australia, Japan

Cover: Foto ©Thomas Meinert / pixelio.de

More available books at **www.hansebooks.com**

COMPANION POETS.

ILLUSTRATED.

LONGFELLOW'S HOUSEHOLD POEMS.

TENNYSON'S SONGS FOR **ALL** SEASONS.

BROWNING'S **LYRICS OF** LIFE.

BOSTON:

JAMES R. OSGOOD AND COMPANY,

LATE TICKNOR & FIELDS, AND FIELDS, OSGOOD, & Co.

1871.

HOUSEHOLD POEMS

BY

HENRY W. LONGFELLOW.

With Illustrations by

JOHN GILBERT, BIRKET FOSTER, AND JOHN ABSOLON.

BOSTON:
TICKNOR AND FIELDS.
1865.

[NOTE. — These selections from the poems of MR. LONGFELLOW are made by the Publishers to supply a demand for all his shorter pieces of a domestic character in a single inexpensive volume of a portable shape.]

UNIVERSITY PRESS:
WELCH, BIGELOW, AND COMPANY,
CAMBRIDGE.

CONTENTS.

iv
CONTENTS.

DEDICATION.

AS one who, walking in the twilight gloom,
    Hears round about him voices as it darkens,
And seeing not the forms from which they come,
    Pauses from time to time, and turns and hearkens,

So walking here in twilight, O my friends!
    I hear your voices, softened by the distance,
And pause, and turn to listen, as each sends
    His words of friendship, comfort, and assistance.

If any thought of mine, or sung or told,
    Has ever given delight or consolation,
Ye have repaid me back a thousand fold,
    By every friendly sign and salutation.

Thanks for the sympathies that ye have shown!
    Thanks for each kindly word, each silent token,
That teaches me, when seeming most alone,
    Friends are around us, though no word be spoken.

Kind messages, that pass from land to land;
    Kind letters, that betray the heart's deep history,
In which **we** feel the pressure of a hand,—
    One touch of fire,—and **all** the rest is mystery!

DEDICATION.

The pleasant books, that silently among
  Our household treasures take familiar places,
And are to us as if a living tongue
  Spake from the printed leaves or pictured faces!

Perhaps on earth I never shall behold,
  With eye of sense, your outward form and semblance;
Therefore to me ye never will grow old,
  But live forever young in my remembrance.

Never grow old, nor change, nor pass away!
  Your gentle voices will flow on forever,
When life grows bare and tarnished with decay,
  As through a leafless landscape flows a river.

Not chance of birth or place has made us friends,
  Being oftentimes of different tongues and nations,
But the endeavor for the selfsame ends,
  With the same hopes, and fears, and aspirations.

Therefore I hope to join your seaside walk,
  Saddened, and mostly silent, with emotion;
Not interrupting with intrusive talk
  The grand, majestic symphonies of ocean.

Therefore I hope, as no unwelcome guest,
  At your warm fireside, when the lamps are lighted,
To have my place reserved among the rest,
  Nor stand as one unsought and uninvited!

HOUSEHOLD POEMS.

HYMN TO THE NIGHT.

'Ασπασίη, τρίλλιστος.

I HEARD the trailing garments of the Night
    Sweep through her marble halls!
I saw her sable skirts all fringed with light
    From the celestial walls!

I felt her presence, by its spell of might,
    Stoop o'er me from above;
The calm, majestic presence of the Night,
    As of the one I love.

I heard the sounds of sorrow and delight,
    The manifold, soft chimes,
That fill the haunted chambers of the Night,
    Like some old poet's rhymes.

From the cool cisterns of the midnight air
    My spirit drank repose;
The fountain of perpetual peace flows there, —
    From those deep cisterns flows.

O holy Night! from thee I learn to bear
    What man has borne before!
Thou layest thy finger on the lips of Care,
    And they complain no more.

Peace! Peace! Orestes-like I breathe this prayer!
  Descend with broad-winged flight,
The welcome, the thrice-prayed for, the most fair,
  The best-beloved Night!

A PSALM OF LIFE.

WHAT THE HEART OF THE YOUNG MAN SAID TO THE PSALMIST.

TELL me not, in mournful numbers,
  "Life is but an empty dream!"
For the soul is dead that slumbers,
  And things are not what they seem.

Life is real! Life is earnest!
  And the grave is not its goal;
"Dust thou art, to dust returnest,"
  Was not spoken of the soul.

Not enjoyment, and not sorrow,
  Is our destined end or way;
But to act, that each to-morrow
  Find us farther than to-day.

Art is long, and Time is fleeting,
  And our hearts, though stout and brave,
Still, like muffled drums, are beating
  Funeral marches to the grave.

In the world's broad field of battle,
  In the bivouac of Life,
Be not like dumb, driven cattle!
  Be a hero in the strife!

Trust no Future, howe'er pleasant!
  Let the dead Past bury its dead!
Act,—act in the living Present!
  Heart within, and God o'erhead!

Lives of great men all remind us
  We can make our lives sublime,
And, departing, leave behind us
  Footprints on the sands of time ;

Footprints, **that** perhaps another,
  Sailing o'er life's solemn main,
A forlorn and shipwrecked brother,
  Seeing, shall take heart again.

Let us, then, be up and doing,
  With a heart for any fate ;
Still achieving, still pursuing,
  Learn to labor and to wait.

THE REAPER AND THE FLOWERS.

THERE is a Reaper, whose name is Death,
  And, with his sickle keen,
He reaps the bearded grain at a breath,
  And the flowers that grow between.

"Shall I have nought that is fair ?" saith he ;
  " Have nought but the bearded grain ?
Though the breath of these flowers is sweet to me,
  I will give them all back again."

He gazed at the flowers with tearful eyes,
  He kissed their drooping leaves ;
It was for the Lord of Paradise
  He bound them in his sheaves.

"**My** Lord has need of these flowerets gay,"
  The Reaper said, and smiled ;
"**Dear** tokens of the earth are they,
  Where he was once a child.

1 *

"They shall all bloom in fields of light,
　Transplanted by my care,
And saints, upon their garments white,
　These sacred blossoms wear."

And the mother gave, in tears and pain,
　The flowers she most did love;
She knew she should find them all again
　In the fields of light above.

O, not in cruelty, not in wrath,
　The Reaper came that day;
'T was an angel visited the green earth,
　And took the flowers away.

THE LIGHT OF STARS.

THE night is come, but not too soon;
    And sinking silently,
All silently, the little moon
    Drops down behind the sky.

There is no light in earth or heaven,
    But the cold light of stars;
And the first watch of night is given
    To the red planet Mars.

Is it the tender star of love?
    The star of love and dreams?
O no! from that blue tent above,
    A hero's armor gleams.

And earnest thoughts within me rise,
    When I behold afar,
Suspended in the evening skies,
    The shield of that red star.

O star of strength! I see thee stand
    And smile upon my pain;
Thou beckonest with thy mailed hand,
    And I am strong again.

Within my breast there is no light,
    But the cold light of stars;
I give the first watch of the night
    To the red planet Mars.

The star of the unconquered will,
    He rises in my breast,
Serene, and resolute, and still,
    And calm, and self-possessed;

And thou, too, whosoe'er thou art,
　That readest this brief psalm,
As one by one thy hopes depart,
　Be resolute and **calm.**

O fear not in a world like this,
　And thou shalt know erelong,
Know how sublime a thing it is
　To suffer and be strong.

FOOTSTEPS OF ANGELS.

WHEN the hours of Day are numbered,
　　And the voices of the Night
Wake the better soul, that slumbered,
　To a holy, calm delight;

Ere the evening lamps are lighted,
　And, like phantoms grim and tall,
Shadows from the fitful fire-light
　Dance upon **the** parlor wall;

Then the forms of the departed
　Enter at the open door;
The beloved, the true-hearted,
　Come to visit me once more;

He, the young and strong, who cherished
　Noble longings for the strife,
By the roadside fell and perished,
　Weary **with** the march of life!

They, the holy ones and weakly,
　Who **the** cross of suffering bore,
Folded their **pale** hands so meekly,
　Spake with us on earth no more!

And with them the Being **Beauteous,**
　Who unto my youth was **given,**

More than all things else to love me,
  And is now **a** saint in heaven.

With a slow and noiseless footstep
  Comes that messenger divine,
Takes the vacant chair beside me,
  Lays her gentle hand in mine.

And she sits and gazes at me
  With those deep and tender eyes,
Like the stars, **so** still and saint-like,
  Looking downward from the skies.

Uttered not, yet comprehended,
  Is the spirit's voiceless prayer,
Soft rebukes, in blessings ended,
  Breathing from her lips of air.

O, though oft depressed and lonely,
  All my fears are laid aside,
If I but remember only
  Such as these have lived and died!

FLOWERS.

S PAKE full well, in language quaint and olden,
  One who dwelleth by the castled Rhine,
When he called the flowers, so blue and golden,
  Stars, that in earth's firmament do shine.

Stars they are, wherein we read our history,
  As astrologers **and seers** of eld;
Yet not wrapped about with awful mystery,
  Like the burning stars, which they beheld.

Wondrous truths, and manifold as wondrous,
  God hath written in those stars above;
But not less in the bright flowerets under **us**
  Stands the revelation of his love.

Bright and glorious is that revelation,
　Written all over this great **world of ours**;
Making evident our own **creation**,
　In these stars of earth, — these golden flowers.

And **the** Poet, faithful and far-seeing,
　Sees, alike in stars and flowers, **a part**
Of the self-same, universal being,
　Which is throbbing in his brain and heart.

Gorgeous flowerets in the sunlight shining,
　Blossoms flaunting in the eye of day,
Tremulous leaves, with soft and silver lining,
　Buds that **open only to decay;**

Brilliant hopes, all woven in gorgeous **tissues**,
　Flaunting gayly in the golden **light**;
Large desires, with most uncertain issues,
　Tender wishes, blossoming at night!

These in flowers **and men** are more **than seeming**,
　Workings are they **of the** self-same **powers**,
Which the Poet, in no idle dreaming,
　Seeth in himself and in the flowers.

Everywhere **about** us are they glowing,
　Some like stars, to tell us Spring is **born**;
Others, their blue eyes with tears o'erflowing,
　Stand like Ruth amid the golden corn;

Not alone in Spring's armorial bearing,
　And in Summer's green-emblazoned field,
But in arms of brave old Autumn's wearing,
　In the centre of his brazen shield;

Not alone in meadows and green alleys,
　On the mountain-top, and by the brink
Of sequestered **pools in woodland** valleys,
　Where the slaves of Nature stoop to drink;

Not alone in her vast dome of glory,
  Not on graves of bird and beast alone,
But in old cathedrals, high and hoary,
  On the tombs of heroes, carved in stone;

In the cottage of the rudest peasant,
  In ancestral homes, whose crumbling towers,
Speaking of the Past unto the Present,
  Tell us of the ancient Games of Flowers;

In all places, then, and in all seasons,
  Flowers expand their light and soul-like wings,
Teaching us, by most persuasive reasons,
  How akin they are to human things.

And with childlike, credulous affection
  We behold their tender buds expand;
Emblems of our own great resurrection,
  Emblems of the bright and better land.

THE BELEAGUERED CITY.

I HAVE read, in some old marvellous tale,
   Some legend strange and vague,
That a midnight host of spectres pale
   Beleaguered the walls of Prague.

Beside the Moldau's rushing stream,
   With the wan moon overhead,
There stood, as in an awful dream,
   The army of the dead.

White as a sea-fog, landward bound,
   The spectral camp was seen,
And, with a sorrowful, deep sound,
   The river flowed between.

No other voice nor sound was there,
   No drum, nor sentry's pace;
The mistlike banners clasped the air,
   As clouds with clouds embrace.

But, when the old cathedral bell
   Proclaimed the morning prayer,
The white pavilions rose and fell
   On the alarmed air.

Down the broad valley fast and far
   The troubled army fled;
Up rose the glorious morning star,
   The ghastly host was dead.

I have read, in the marvellous heart of man,
   That strange and mystic scroll,
That an army of phantoms vast and wan
   Beleaguer the human soul.

Encamped beside Life's rushing **stream,**
  In Fancy's misty light,
Gigantic shapes and shadows gleam
  Portentous through the night.

Upon its midnight battle-ground
  The spectral camp is seen,
And, with a sorrowful, deep sound,
  Flows the River of Life between.

No other voice, nor sound is there,
  In the army of the grave;
No other challenge breaks the air,
  But the rushing of Life's wave.

And, **when** the solemn and **deep** church-bell
  Entreats the soul to pray,
The midnight phantoms feel the spell,
  The shadows sweep away.

Down the broad **Vale of Tears afar**
  The spectral camp is fled;
Faith shineth as a morning star,
  Our ghastly fears are dead.

MIDNIGHT MASS FOR THE DYING YEAR.

YES, **the** Year is growing old,
  And his eye is pale and bleared!
Death, with frosty hand and cold,
  Plucks the old man by the beard,
      Sorely, — sorely!

The leaves are falling, falling,
  Solemnly and slow;
Caw! caw! the rooks are calling,
  It is a sound of woe,
      A sound of woe!

Through woods and mountain passes
  The winds, like anthems, roll;
They are chanting solemn masses,
  Singing; "Pray for this poor soul,
    Pray, — pray!"

And the hooded clouds, like friars,
  Tell their beads in drops of rain,
And patter their doleful prayers! —
  But their prayers are all in vain,
    All in vain!

There he stands in the foul weather,
  The foolish, fond Old Year,
Crowned with wild flowers and with heather,
  Like weak, despised Lear,
    A king, — a king!

Then comes the summer-like day,
  Bids the old man rejoice!
His joy! his last! O, the old man gray,
  Loveth that ever-soft voice,
    Gentle and low.

To the crimson woods he saith, —
  To the voice gentle and low
Of the soft air, like a daughter's breath, —
  "Pray do not mock me so!
    Do not laugh at me!"

And now the sweet day is dead;
  Cold in his arms it lies;
No stain from its breath is spread
  Over the glassy skies,
    No mist or stain!

Then, too, the Old Year dieth,
  And the forests utter a moan,
Like the voice of one who crieth
  In the wilderness alone,
    "Vex not his ghost!"

Then comes, with an awful roar,
   Gathering and sounding on,
The storm-wind from Labrador,
   The wind Euroclydon,
     The storm-wind!

Howl! howl! and from the forest
   Sweep the red leaves away!
Would, the sins that thou abhorrest,
   O Soul! could thus decay,
     And be swept away!

For there shall come a mightier blast,
   There shall be a darker day;
And the stars, from heaven down-cast,
   Like red leaves be swept away!
     Kyrie, eleyson!
     Christe, eleyson!

THE RAINY DAY.

THE day is cold, and dark, and dreary;
  It rains, and the wind is never weary;
The vine still clings to the mouldering wall,
But at every gust the dead leaves fall,
    And the day is dark and dreary.

My life is cold, and dark, and dreary;
It rains, and the wind is never weary;
My thoughts still cling to the mouldering Past,
But the hopes of youth fall thick in the blast,
    And the days are dark and dreary.

Be still, sad heart! and cease repining;
Behind the clouds is the sun still shining;
Thy fate is the common fate of all,
Into each life some rain must fall,   .
    Some days must be dark and dreary.

IT IS NOT ALWAYS MAY.

NO HAY PÁJAROS EN LOS NIDOS DE ANTAÑO.
                               Spanish Proverb.

THE sun is bright, — the air is clear,
  The darting swallows soar and sing,
And from the stately elms I hear
  The blue-bird prophesying Spring.

So blue yon winding river flows,
  It seems an outlet from the sky,
Where waiting till the west wind blows,
  The freighted clouds at anchor lie.

All things are new; — the buds, **the leaves,**
  That gild the elm-tree's nodding crest,
And even the nest beneath the eaves; —
  There are no birds in last year's nest!

All things rejoice in youth and love,
  The fulness of their first delight!
And learn from the soft heavens above
  The melting tenderness of night.

Maiden, **that** read'st this simple rhyme,
  Enjoy thy youth, it will not stay;
Enjoy the fragrance of thy prime,
  For O! it is not always May!

Enjoy the Spring of Love and Youth,
  To some good angel leave **the rest;**
For Time will teach thee **soon the truth,**
  There are no birds in last year's nest!

.

THE VILLAGE BLACKSMITH.

U NDER a spreading **chestnut-tree**
  The village smithy stands;
The smith, a mighty man is he,
  With large and sinewy hands;
And the muscles of his brawny arms
  Are strong as iron bands.

His hair is crisp, and black, and long,
  His face is like the tan;
His brow is wet with honest sweat,
  He earns whate'er he can,
And looks the whole world in the face,
  For he owes not any **man.**

Week in, week out, from morn till night,
    You can hear his bellows blow;
You can hear him swing his heavy sledge,
    With measured beat and slow,
Like a sexton ringing the village bell,
    When the evening sun is low.

And children coming home from school
    Look in at the open door;
They love to see the flaming forge,
    And hear the bellows roar,
And catch the burning sparks that fly
    Like chaff from a threshing floor.

He goes on Sunday to the church,
    And sits among his boys;
He hears the parson pray and preach,
    He hears his daughter's voice,
Singing in the village choir,
    And it makes his heart rejoice.

It sounds to him like her mother's voice,
    Singing in Paradise!
He needs must think of her once more,
    How in the grave she lies;
And with his hard, rough hand he wipes
    A tear out of his eyes.

Toiling, — rejoicing, — sorrowing,
  Onward through life he goes ;
Each morning sees some task begin,
  Each evening sees it close ;
Something attempted, something done,
  Has earned a night's repose.

Thanks, thanks to thee, my worthy **friend,**
  For the lesson thou hast taught!
Thus at the flaming forge of life
  Our fortunes must be wrought ;
Thus on its sounding anvil shaped
  Each burning deed and thought!

GOD'S-ACRE.

I LIKE **that ancient Saxon** phrase, **which calls**
  The burial-ground God's-Acre ! It is just ;
It consecrates each grave within its walls,
  And breathes a benison o'er the sleeping dust.

God's-Acre ! Yes, that blessed name **imparts**
  Comfort to those, who in the grave have sown
The seed, that they had garnered in their hearts,
  Their bread of life, alas ! no more their own.

Into its furrows shall we all be cast,
  'In the sure faith, that **we** shall rise again
At the great harvest, **when the** archangel's **blast**
  Shall winnow, like **a fan, the chaff and grain.**

Then shall the good stand in immortal bloom,
  In the fair gardens of that second birth ;
And each bright blossom, mingle its perfume
  With that of flowers, which never bloomed on earth.

With thy rude ploughshare, Death, turn up the sod,
  And spread the furrow for the seed we sow;
This is the field and Acre of **our God,**
  This is the place where human harvests grow!

TO THE RIVER CHARLES.

RIVER! that in silence windest
    Through the meadows, bright and free,
Till at length thy rest thou findest
  In the bosom of the sea!

Four long years of mingled feeling,
  Half in rest, and half in strife,
I have seen thy waters stealing
  Onward, like the stream of life.

Thou hast taught me, **Silent River!**
  Many a lesson, deep and **long;**
Thou hast been a generous **giver;**
  I can give thee but a song.

Oft in sadness and in illness
  I have watched thy current glide,
Till the beauty of its stillness
  Overflowed me, like a tide.

And in better hours and brighter,
  When I saw thy waters gleam,
I have felt my heart beat lighter,
  And leap onward **with** thy **stream.**

Not for this alone I love thee,
  Nor because thy waves of blue
From celestial seas above thee
  Take their own celestial hue.

Where yon shadowy woodlands hide thee,
  And thy waters disappear,
Friends I love have dwelt beside thee,
  And have made thy margin dear.

More than this ; — thy name reminds me
  Of three friends, all true and tried ;
And that name, like magic, binds me
  Closer, closer, to thy side.

Friends my soul with joy remembers !
  How like quivering flames they start,
When I fan the living embers
  On the hearth-stone of my heart !

'T is for this, thou Silent River !
  That my spirit leans to thee ;
Thou hast been a generous giver,
  Take this idle song from me.

THE GOBLET OF LIFE.

FILLED is Life's goblet to the brim ;
  And though my eyes with tears are dim,
I see its sparkling bubbles swim,
And chant a melancholy hymn
  With solemn voice and slow.

No purple flowers, — no garlands green,
Conceal the goblet's shade or sheen,
Nor maddening draughts of Hippocrene,
Like gleams of sunshine, flash between
  Thick leaves of mistletoe.

This goblet, wrought with curious art,
Is filled with waters, that upstart,
When the deep fountains of the heart,
By strong convulsions rent apart,
  Are running all to waste.

2

And as it mantling passes round,
With fennel is it wreathed and crowned,
Whose seed and foliage sun-imbrowned
Are in its waters steeped and drowned,
    And give a bitter taste.

Above the lowly plants it towers,
The fennel, with its yellow flowers,
And in an earlier age than ours
Was gifted with the wondrous powers,
    Lost vision to restore.

It gave new strength, and fearless mood;
And gladiators, fierce and rude,
Mingled it in their daily food;
And he who battled and subdued,
    A wreath of fennel wore.

Then in Life's goblet freely press,
The leaves that give it bitterness,
Nor prize the colored waters less,
For in thy darkness and distress
    New light and strength they give!

And he who has not learned to know
How false its sparkling bubbles show,
How bitter are the drops of woe,
With which its brim may overflow,
    He has not learned to live.

The prayer of Ajax was for light;
Through all that dark and desperate fight,
The blackness of that noonday night,
He asked but the return of sight,
    To see his foeman's face.

Let our unceasing, earnest prayer
Be, too, for light, — for strength to bear
Our portion of the weight of care,
That crushes into dumb despair
    One half the human race.

MAIDENHOOD.

O suffering, sad humanity!
O ye afflicted ones, who lie
Steeped to the lips in misery,
Longing, and yet afraid to die,
    Patient, though sorely **tried**!

I pledge you in this cup of grief,
Where floats the fennel's bitter leaf,
The Battle of our Life is brief,
The alarm, — the struggle, — the relief, —
    Then sleep we side by side.

MAIDENHOOD.

M AIDEN! with the meek, brown eyes,
    In whose **orbs a shadow lies**
Like the dusk in **evening skies**!

Thou whose locks outshine the **sun,**
Golden tresses, wreathed **in one,**
As the braided streamlets run!

Standing, with reluctant feet,
Where the brook and river meet,
Womanhood and childhood fleet!

Gazing, with a timid glance,
On **the** brooklet's swift advance,
On the river's broad expanse!

Deep and still, that gliding stream
Beautiful to thee must seem,
As the river of a dream.

Then why pause with indecision,
When bright angels in thy vision
Beckon thee to fields Elysian?

Seest thou shadows sailing by,
As the dove, with startled eye,
Sees the falcon's shadow fly?

Hearest thou voices on the shore,
That our ears perceive no more,
Deafened by the cataract's roar?

O, thou child of many prayers!
Life hath quicksands, — Life hath snares, —
Care and age come unawares!

Like the swell of some sweet tune,
Morning rises into noon,
May glides onward into June.

Childhood is the bough, where slumbered
Birds and blossoms many-numbered; —
Age, that bough with snows encumbered.

Gather, then, each flower that grows,
When the young heart overflows,
To embalm that tent of snows.

Bear a lily in thy hand;
Gates of brass cannot withstand
One touch of that magic wand.

Bear through sorrow, wrong, and ruth,
In thy heart the dew of youth,
On thy lips the smile of truth.

O, that dew, like balm, shall steal
Into wounds, that cannot heal,
Even as sleep our eyes doth seal;

And that smile, like sunshine, dart
Into many a sunless heart,
For a smile of God thou art.

THE shades of night were falling fast,
As through an Alpine village passed
A youth, who bore, 'mid snow and ice,
A banner with the strange device,
Excelsior !

His brow was sad; his eye beneath,
Flashed like a faulchion from its sheath,
And like a silver clarion rung
The accents of that unknown tongue,
Excelsior !

In happy homes he saw the light
Of household fires gleam warm and bright;
Above, the spectral glaciers shone,
And from his lips escaped a groan,
Excelsior !

"Try not the Pass!" the old man said;
"Dark lowers the tempest overhead,.
The roaring torrent is deep and wide!"
And loud that clarion voice replied,
     Excelsior!

"O stay," the maiden said, "and rest
Thy weary head upon this breast!"
A tear stood in his bright blue **eye**,
But still he answered, with **a sigh**,
     Excelsior!

"**Beware the pine-tree's withered branch!**
Beware **the awful avalanche!**"
This was the peasant's **last** Good-night,
A voice replied, **far up the** height,
     Excelsior! ·

At break of day, **as** heavenward
The pious monks **of** Saint Bernard
Uttered the oft-repeated prayer,
A voice cried through the startled air,
     Excelsior!

A traveller, by **the** faithful hound,
Half-buried in **the** snow was found,
Still grasping **in** his hand of ice
That banner with **the strange device**,
     Excelsior!

There in the twilight cold and **gray**,
Lifeless, but beautiful, he lay,
And from the sky, serene and far,
A voice fell, like **a falling** star,
     Excelsior!

A GLEAM OF SUNSHINE.

THIS is the place. Stand still, my steed,
  Let me review the scene,
And summon from the shadowy Past
  The forms that once have been.

The Past and Present here unite
  Beneath Time's flowing tide,
Like footprints hidden by a brook,
  But seen on either side.

Here runs the highway to the town;
  There the green lane descends,
Through which I walked to church with thee,
  O gentlest of my friends!

The shadow of the linden-trees,
  Lay moving on the grass;
Between them and the moving boughs,
  A shadow, thou didst pass.

Thy dress was like the lilies,
  And thy heart as pure as they:
One of God's holy messengers
  Did walk with me that day.

I saw the branches of the trees
  Bend down thy touch to meet,
The clover-blossoms in the grass
  Rise up to kiss thy feet.

"Sleep, sleep to-day, tormenting cares,
  Of earth and folly born!"
Solemnly sang the village choir
  On that sweet Sabbath morn.

Through the closed blinds the golden sun
  Poured in a dusty beam,
Like the celestial ladder seen
  By Jacob in his dream.

And ever and anon, the wind,
  Sweet-scented with the hay,
Turned o'er the hymn-book's fluttering leaves
  That on the window lay.

Long was the good man's sermon,
  Yet it seemed not so to me;
For he spake of Ruth the beautiful,
  And still I thought of thee.

Long was the prayer he uttered,
  Yet it seemed not so to me;
For in my heart I prayed with him,
  And still I thought of thee.

But now, alas! the place seems changed;
  Thou art no longer here:
Part of the sunshine of the scene
  With thee did disappear.

Though thoughts, deep-rooted in my heart,
  Like pine-trees dark and high,
Subdue the light of noon, and breathe
  A low and ceaseless sigh;

This memory brightens o'er the past,
  As when the sun, concealed
Behind some cloud that near us hangs,
  Shines on a distant field.

RAIN IN SUMMER.

HOW beautiful is the rain!
  After the dust and heat,
In the broad and fiery street,
In the narrow lane,
How beautiful **is** the rain!

How it clatters along the roofs,
Like the tramp of hoofs!
How it gushes and struggles out
From the throat of the overflowing spout!
Across the window-pane
It pours and pours;
And swift and wide,
With a muddy tide,
Like a river down the gutter roars
The rain, the welcome rain!

The sick man from his chamber looks
At the twisted brooks;
He can feel the cool
Breath of each little pool;
His fevered brain
Grows calm again,
And he breathes a blessing on **the rain.**

From the neighboring school
Come the boys,
With more than their **wonted noise**
And commotion;
And down the wet streets
Sail their mimic fleets,
Till the treacherous pool
Engulfs them in **its** whirling
And turbulent ocean.

2 *   C

In the country, on every side,
Where, far and wide,
Like a leopard's tawny and spotted hide,
Stretches the plain,
To the dry grass and the drier grain
How welcome is the rain!

In the furrowed land
The toilsome and patient oxen stand;
Lifting the yoke-encumbered head,
With their dilated nostrils spread,
They silently inhale
The clover-scented gale,
And the vapors that arise
From the well watered and smoking soil.
For this rest in the furrow after toil
Their large and lustrous eyes
Seem to thank the Lord,
More than man's spoken word.

Near at hand,
From under the sheltering trees,
The farmer sees
His pastures, and his fields of grain,
As they bend their tops
To the numberless beating drops
Of the incessant rain.
He counts it as no sin
That he sees therein
Only his own thrift and gain.
These, and far more than these,
The Poet sees!
He can behold
Aquarius old
Walking the fenceless fields of air;
And from each ample fold
Of the clouds about him rolled
Scattering everywhere
The showery rain,
As the farmer scatters his grain.

He can behold
Things manifold
That have not yet been wholly told,
Have not been wholly sung nor said.
For his thought, that never stops,
Follows the water-drops
Down to the graves of **the dead,**
Down through chasms and gulfs profound,
To the dreary fountain-head
Of lakes and rivers under ground;
And sees them, when the rain is done,
On the bridge **of** colors seven
Climbing up once more to heaven,
Opposite the setting sun.

Thus the Seer,
With vision clear,
Sees forms appear and disappear,
In the perpetual round of strange,
Mysterious change
From birth to death, from death to birth,
From earth to heaven, from heaven to earth;
Till glimpses more sublime
Of things, unseen before,
Unto his wondering eyes reveal
The Universe, as an immeasurable wheel
Turning forevermore
In the rapid and rushing river of Time.

TO A CHILD.

DEAR child! how radiant on thy mother's **knee,**
With merry-making eyes and jocund smiles,
Thou gazest at the painted tiles,
Whose **figures grace,**
With many **a** grotesque form and face,

The ancient chimney of thy nursery!
The lady with the gay macaw,
The dancing girl, the grave bashaw
With bearded lip and chin;
And, leaning idly o'er his gate,
Beneath the imperial fan of state,
The Chinese mandarin.

With what a look of proud command
Thou shakest in thy little hand
The coral rattle with its silver bells,
Making a merry tune!
Thousands of years in Indian seas
That coral grew, by slow degrees,
Until some deadly and wild monsoon
Dashed it on Coromandel's sand!
Those silver bells
Reposed of yore,
As shapeless ore,
Far down in the deep-sunken wells
Of darksome mines,
In some obscure and sunless place,
Beneath huge Chimborazo's base,
Or Potosí's o'erhanging pines!
And thus for thee, O little child,
Through many a danger and escape,
The tall ships passed the stormy cape;
For thee in foreign lands remote,
Beneath the burning, tropic clime,
The Indian peasant, chasing the wild goat,
Himself as swift and wild,
In falling, clutched the frail arbute,
The fibres of whose shallow root,
Uplifted from the soil, betrayed
The silver veins beneath it laid,
The buried treasures of the pirate, Time.

But, lo! thy door is left ajar!
Thou hearest footsteps from afar!

And, at the sound,
Thou turnest round
With quick and questioning eyes,
Like one, who, in a foreign land,
Beholds on every hand
Some source of wonder and surprise!
And, restlessly, impatiently,
Thou strivest, strugglest, to be free.
The four walls of thy nursery
Are now like prison walls to thee.
No more thy mother's smiles,
No more the painted tiles,
Delight thee, nor the playthings on the floor
That won thy little, beating heart before;
Thou strugglest for the open door.

Through these once solitary halls
Thy pattering footstep falls.
The sound of thy merry voice
Makes the old walls
Jubilant, and they rejoice
With the joy of thy young heart,
O'er the light of whose gladness
No shadows of sadness
From the sombre background of memory start.

Once, ah, once, within these walls,
One whom memory oft recalls,
The Father of his Country, dwelt.
And yonder meadows, broad and damp,
The fires of the besieging camp
Encircled with a burning belt.
Up and down these echoing stairs,
Heavy with the weight of cares,
Sounded his majestic tread;
Yes, within this very room
Sat he in those hours of gloom,
Weary both in heart and head.

But what are these grave thoughts to thee?
Out, out! into the open air!
Thy only dream is liberty,
Thou carest little how or where.
I see thee eager at thy play,
Now shouting to the apples on the tree,
With cheeks as round and red as they;
And now among the yellow stalks,
Among the flowering shrubs and plants,
As restless as the bee.
Along the garden walks,
The tracks of thy small carriage-wheels I trace;
And see at every turn how they efface
Whole villages of sand-roofed tents,
That rise like golden domes
Above the cavernous and secret homes
Of wandering and nomadic tribes of ants.
Ah, cruel little Tamerlane,
Who, with thy dreadful reign,
Dost persecute and overwhelm
These hapless Troglodytes of thy realm!

What! tired already! with those suppliant looks,
And voice more beautiful than a poet's books,
Or murmuring sound of water as it flows,
'Thou comest back to parley with repose!

TO A CHILD.

This rustic seat in the old apple-tree,
With its o'erhanging golden canopy
Of leaves illuminate with autumnal hues,
And shining with the argent light of dews,
Shall for a season be our place of rest.
Beneath us, like an oriole's pendent nest,
From which the laughing birds have taken wing,
By thee abandoned, hangs thy vacant swing.
Dream-like the waters of the river gleam;
A sailless vessel drops adown the stream,
And like it, to a sea as wide and deep,
Thou driftest gently down the tides of sleep.

O child! O new-born denizen
Of life's great city! on thy head
The glory of the morn is shed,
Like a celestial benison!
Here at the portal thou dost stand,
And with thy little hand
Thou openest the mysterious gate
Into the future's undiscovered land.
I see its valves expand,
As at the touch of Fate!
Into those realms of love and hate,
Into that darkness, blank and drear,
By some prophetic feeling taught,
I launch the bold, adventurous thought,
Freighted with hope and fear;
As upon subterranean streams,
In caverns unexplored and dark,
Men sometimes launch a fragile bark,
Laden with flickering fire,
And watch its swift-receding beams,
Until at length they disappear,
And in the distant dark expire.
By what astrology of fear or hope
Dare I to cast thy horoscope!
Like the new moon thy life appears;
A little strip of silver light,

And widening outward into night
The shadowy disk of future years;
And yet upon its outer rim,
A luminous circle, faint and dim,
And scarcely visible to us here,
Rounds and completes the perfect sphere;
A prophecy and intimation,
A pale and feeble adumbration,
Of the great world of light, that lies
Behind all human destinies.

Ah! if thy fate, with anguish fraught,
Should be to wet the dusty soil
With the hot tears and sweat of toil, —
To struggle with imperious thought,
Until the overburdened brain,
Weary with labor, faint with pain,
Like a jarred pendulum, retain
Only its motion, not its power, —
Remember, in that perilous hour,
When most afflicted and oppressed,
From labor there shall come forth rest.

'And if a more auspicious fate
On thy advancing steps await,
Still let it ever be thy pride
To linger by the laborer's side;
With words of sympathy or song
To cheer the dreary march along
Of the great army of the poor,
O'er desert sand, o'er dangerous moor.

Nor to thyself the task shall be
Without reward; for thou shalt learn
The wisdom early to discern
True beauty in utility;
As great Pythagoras of yore,
Standing beside the blacksmith's door,
And hearing the hammers, as they smote

The anvils with a different note,
Stole from the varying tones, that hung
Vibrant on every iron tongue,
The secret of the sounding wire,
And formed the seven-chorded **lyre.**

Enough! I will not play the **Seer**;
I will no longer strive to ope
The mystic volume, where appear
The herald Hope, forerunning Fear,
And Fear, the pursuivant of Hope.
Thy destiny remains untold;
For, like Acestes' shaft of old,
The swift thought kindles as it **flies,**
And burns to ashes in the skies.

THE BRIDGE.

I STOOD on the bridge at midnight,
   As the clocks were striking the hour,
And the moon **rose** o'er the city,
   Behind the dark church-tower.

I saw her bright reflection
   In the waters under me,
Like a golden goblet falling
   And sinking into the sea.

And far in the hazy distance
   Of that lovely night in June,
The blaze of the flaming furnace
   Gleamed redder than the **moon.**

Among the long, black rafters
   The wavering shadows lay,
And the current that came from the ocean
   Seemed to lift and bear them away;

As, sweeping and eddying through them,
  Rose the belated tide,
And, streaming into the moonlight,
  The sea-weed floated wide.

And like those waters rushing
  Among the wooden piers,
A flood of thoughts came o'er me
  That filled my eyes with tears.

How often, O, how often,
  In the days that had gone by,
I had stood on that bridge at midnight
  And gazed on that wave and sky!

How often, O, how often,
  I had wished that the ebbing tide
Would bear me away on its bosom
  O'er the ocean wild and wide!

For my heart was hot and restless,
  And my life was full of care,
And the burden laid upon me
  Seemed greater than I could bear.

But now it has fallen from me,
  It is buried in the sea;
And only the sorrow of others
  Throws it shadow over me.

Yet whenever I cross the river
  On its bridge with wooden piers,
Like the odor of brine from the ocean
  Comes the thought of other years.

And I think how many thousands
  Of care-encumbered men,
Each bearing his burden of sorrow,
  Have crossed the bridge since then.

I see the long procession
  Still passing to and fro,
The young heart hot and restless,
  And the old subdued and slow!

And forever and forever,
  As long as the river flows,
As long as the heart has passions,
  As long as life has **woes**;

The moon and its broken reflection
  And its shadows shall appear,
As the symbol of love in heaven,
  And its wavering image here.

SEA-WEED.

WHEN descends on the Atlantic
    The gigantic
Storm-wind of the equinox,
Landward in his wrath he scourges
    The toiling surges,
Laden with sea-weed from the rocks:

From Bermuda's reefs; from edges
    Of sunken ledges,
In some far-off, bright Azore;
From Bahama, and the dashing,
    Silver-flashing
Surges of San Salvador;

From the tumbling surf, that buries
    The **Orkneyan** skerries,
Answering the hoarse **Hebrides**;
And from wrecks of ships, and drifting
    Spars, uplifting
On the desolate, rainy seas; —

Ever drifting, drifting, drifting
    On the shifting
Currents of the restless main;
Till in sheltered coves, and reaches
    Of sandy beaches,
All have found repose again.

So when storms of wild emotion
    Strike the ocean
Of the poet's soul, erelong
From each cave and rocky fastness,
    In its vastness,
Floats some fragment of a song:

From the far-off isles enchanted,
    Heaven has planted
With the golden fruit of Truth;
From the flashing surf, whose vision
    Gleams Elysian
In the tropic clime of Youth;

From the strong Will, and the Endeavor
    That forever
Wrestles with the tides of Fate;
From the wreck of Hopes far-scattered,
    Tempest-shattered,
Floating waste and desolate; —

Ever drifting, drifting, drifting
    On the shifting
Currents of the restless heart;
Till at length in books recorded,
    They, like hoarded
Household words, no more depart.

AFTERNOON IN FEBRUARY.

THE day is ending,
    The night is descending;
The marsh is frozen,
    The river dead.

Through clouds like ashes
The red sun flashes
On village windows
    That glimmer red.

The snow recommences;
The buried fences
Mark no longer
    The road o'er the plain;

While through the meadows,
Like fearful shadows,
Slowly passes
   A funeral train.

The bell is pealing,
And every feeling
Within me responds
   To the dismal knell;

Shadows are trailing,
My heart is bewailing
And tolling within
   Like a funeral bell.

THE DAY IS DONE.

THE day is done, and the darkness
   Falls from the wings of Night,
As a feather is wafted downward
   From an eagle in his flight.

I see the lights of the village
   Gleam through the rain and the mist,
And a feeling of sadness comes o'er me,
   That my soul cannot resist :

A feeling of sadness and longing,
   That is not akin to pain,
And resembles sorrow only
   As the mist resembles the rain.

Come, read to me some poem,
   Some simple and heartfelt lay,
That shall soothe this restless feeling,
   And banish the thoughts of day.

Not from the grand old masters,
   Not from the bards sublime,
Whose distant footsteps echo
   Through the corridors of **Time.**

For, like strains of martial music,
   Their mighty thoughts suggest
Life's endless toil and endeavor;
   And to-night I long for rest.

Read from some humbler poet,
   Whose songs gushed from his heart,
As showers from the clouds of summer,
   Or tears from the eyelids start;

Who, through **long days of labor,**
   And nights **devoid of ease,**
Still heard **in** his **soul** the music
   Of wonderful melodies.

Such songs have power to **quiet**
   The restless pulse of **care,**
And come like the benediction
   That follows after prayer.

Then read from the treasured volume
   The poem of thy choice,
And lend to the rhyme of **the poet**
   The beauty of thy voice.

And the night shall **be** filled with music,
   And the cares, that infest the day,
Shall fold their tents, like the Arabs,
   And as silently steal away.

THE ARROW AND THE SONG.

I SHOT an arrow into the air,
It fell to earth, I knew not where;
For, so swiftly it flew, the sight
Could not follow it in its flight.

I breathed a song into the air,
It fell to earth, I knew not where;
For who has sight so keen and strong,
That it can follow the flight of song?

Long, long afterward, in an oak
I found the arrow, still unbroke;
And the song, from beginning to end,
I found again in the heart of a friend.

THE OLD CLOCK ON THE STAIRS.

L'éternité est une pendule, dont le balancier dit et redit sans cesse ces
deux mots seulement, dans le silence des tombeaux: "Toujours! jamais!
Jamais! toujours!"

JACQUES BRIDAINE.

SOMEWHAT back from the village street
Stands the old-fashioned country-seat.
Across its antique portico
Tall poplar-trees their shadows throw,
And from its station in the hall
An ancient timepiece says to all, —
        "Forever — never!
        Never — forever!"

Half-way up the stairs it stands,
And points and beckons with its hands
From its case of massive oak,
Like a monk, who, under his cloak,
Crosses himself, and sighs, alas !
With sorrowful voice to all who pass, —
      " Forever — never !
      Never — forever ! "

3   D

By day its voice is low and light;
But in the silent dead of night,
Distinct as a passing footstep's fall,
It echoes along the vacant hall,
Along the ceiling, along the floor,
And seems to say, at each chamber-door, —
    " Forever — never!
    Never — forever! "

Through days of sorrow and of mirth,
Through days of death and days of birth,
Through every swift vicissitude
Of changeful time, unchanged it has stood,
And as if, like God, it all things saw,
It calmly repeats those words of awe, —
    " Forever — never!
    Never — forever! "

In that mansion used to be .
Free-hearted Hospitality;
His great fires up the chimney roared;
The stranger feasted at his board;
But, like the skeleton at the feast,
That warning timepiece never ceased, —
    " Forever — never!
    Never — forever! "

There groups of merry children played,
There youths and maidens dreaming strayed.
O precious hours! O golden prime,
And affluence of love and time!
Even as a miser counts his gold,
Those hours the ancient timepiece told, —
    " Forever — never!
    Never — forever! "

From that chamber, clothed in white,
The bride came forth on her wedding night;
There, in that silent room below,
The dead lay in his shroud of snow;

And in the hush that followed the prayer,
Was heard the old clock on the stair, —
    " Forever — never !
    Never — forever ! "

All are scattered now and fled,
Some are married, some are dead ;
And when I ask, with throbs of pain,
" Ah ! when shall they all meet again ?
As in the days long-since gone by,
The ancient timepiece makes reply, —
    " Forever — never !
    Never — forever ! "

Never here, forever there,
Where all parting, pain, and care,
And death, and time shall disappear, —
Forever there, but never here !
The horologe of Eternity
Sayeth this incessantly, —
    " Forever — never !
    Never — forever ! "

THE EVENING STAR.

LO ! in the painted oriel of **the West**,
  Whose panes the sunken sun incarnadines,
Like a fair lady at her casement, shines
The evening star, the star of love and rest !
And then anon she doth herself divest
Of all her **radiant** garments, and reclines
Behind the sombre screen of yonder pines,
With slumber and soft dreams of love oppressed.
O **my** beloved, my sweet Hesperus !
My morning and my evening star of love !

My best and gentlest lady! even thus,
As that fair planet in the sky above,
Dost thou retire unto thy rest at night,
And from thy darkened window fades the light.

AUTUMN.

THOU comest, Autumn, heralded by the rain,
    With banners, by great gales incessant fanned,
Brighter than brightest silks of Samarcand,
And stately oxen harnessed to thy wain!
Thou standest, like imperial Charlemagne,
Upon thy bridge of gold; thy royal hand
Outstretched with benedictions o'er the land,
Blessing the farms through all thy vast domain.
Thy shield is the red harvest moon, suspended
So long beneath the heaven's o'erhanging eaves,
Thy steps are by the farmer's prayers attended;
Like flames upon an altar shine the sheaves;
And, following thee, in thy ovation splendid,
Thine almoner, the wind, scatters the golden leaves!

THE SECRET OF THE SEA.

AH! what pleasant visions haunt me
    As I gaze upon the sea!
All the old romantic legends,
    All my dreams, come back to me.

Sails of silk and ropes of sendal,
    Such as gleam in ancient lore;
And the singing of the sailors,
    And the answer from the shore!

Most of all, the Spanish ballad
    Haunts me oft, and tarries long,
Of the noble Count Arnaldos
    And the sailor's mystic song.

Like the long waves on a sea-beach,
    Where the sand as silver shines,
With a soft, monotonous cadence,
    Flow its unrhymed lyric lines ; —

Telling how the Count Arnaldos,
    With his hawk upon his hand,
Saw a fair and stately galley,
    Steering onward to the land ; —

How he heard the ancient helmsman
    Chant a song so wild and clear,
That the sailing sea-bird slowly
    Poised upon the mast to hear,

Till his soul was full of longing,
    And he cried, with impulse strong, —
" Helmsman ! for the love of heaven,
    Teach me, too, that wondrous song ! "

" Wouldst thou," — so the helmsman answered,
    " Learn the secret of the sea ?
Only those who brave its dangers
    Comprehend its mystery ! "

In each sail that skims the horizon,
    In each landward-blowing breeze,
I behold that stately galley,
    Hear those mournful melodies ;

Till my soul is full of longing
    For the secret of the sea,
And the heart of the great ocean
    Sends a thrilling pulse through me.

TWILIGHT.

THE twilight is sad and cloudy,
  The wind blows wild and free,
And like the wings of sea-birds
  Flash the white caps of the sea.

But in the fisherman's cottage
  There shines a ruddier light,
And a little face at the window
  Peers out into the night.

Close, close it is pressed to the window,
  As if those childish eyes
Were looking into the darkness,
  To see some form arise.

And a woman's waving shadow
  Is passing to and fro,
Now rising to the ceiling,
  Now bowing and bending low.

What tale do the roaring ocean,
　And the night-wind, bleak and wild,
As they beat at the crazy casement,
　Tell to that little child?

And why do the roaring ocean,
　And the night-wind, wild and bleak,
As they beat at the heart of the mother,
　Drive the color from her cheek?

THE LIGHTHOUSE.

THE rocky ledge runs far into the sea,
　And on its outer point, some miles away,
The Lighthouse lifts its massive masonry,
　A pillar of fire by night, of cloud by day.

Even at this distance I can see the tides,
　Upheaving, break unheard along its base,
A speechless wrath, that rises and subsides
　In the white lip and tremor of the face.

And as the evening darkens, lo! how bright,
　Through the deep purple of the twilight air,
Beams forth the sudden radiance of its light,
　With strange, unearthly splendor in its glare!

Not one alone; from each projecting cape
　And perilous reef along the ocean's verge,
Starts into life a dim, gigantic shape,
　Holding its lantern o'er the restless surge.

Like the great giant Christopher it stands
　Upon the brink of the tempestuous wave,
Wading far out among the rocks and sands,
　The night-o'ertaken mariner to save.

And the great ships sail outward and return,
  Bending and bowing o'er the billowy swells,
And ever joyful, as they see it burn,
  They wave their silent welcomes and farewells.

They come forth from the darkness, and their sails
  Gleam for a moment only in the blaze,
And eager faces, as the light unveils,
  Gaze at the tower, and vanish while they gaze.

The mariner remembers when a child,
  On his first voyage, he saw it fade and sink;
And when, returning from adventures wild,
  He saw it rise again o'er ocean's brink.

Steadfast, serene, immovable, the same
  Year after year, through all the silent night,
Burns on forevermore that quenchless flame,
  Shines on that inextinguishable light!

It sees the ocean to its bosom clasp
  The rocks and sea-sand with the kiss of peace;
It sees the wild winds lift it in their grasp,
  And hold it up, and shake it like a fleece.

The startled waves leap over it; the storm
  Smites it with all the scourges of the rain,
And steadily against its solid form
  Press the great shoulders of the hurricane.

The sea-bird wheeling round it, with the din
  Of wings and winds and solitary cries,
Blinded and maddened by the light within,
  Dashes himself against the glare, and dies.

A new Prometheus, chained upon the rock,
  Still grasping in his hand the fire of Jove,
It does not hear the cry, nor heed the shock,
  But hails the mariner with words of love.

" Sail on ! " it says, " sail on, ye stately ships !
    And with your floating bridge the ocean span ;
Be mine to guard this light from all eclipse,
    Be yours to bring man nearer unto man ! "

THE FIRE OF DRIFT-WOOD.

WE sat within the farm-house old,
        Whose windows, looking o'er the bay,
Gave to the sea-breeze, damp and cold,
    An easy entrance, night and day.

Not far away we saw the port, —
    The strange, old-fashioned, silent town, —
The lighthouse, the dismantled fort, —
    The wooden houses, quaint and brown.

We sat and talked until the night,
    Descending, filled the little room ;
Our faces faded from the sight,
    Our voices only broke the gloom.

We spake of many a vanished scene,
    Of what we once had thought and said,
Of what had been, and might have been,
    And who was changed, and who was dead ;

And all that fills the hearts of friends,
    When first they feel, with secret pain,
Their lives thenceforth have separate ends,
    And never can be one again ;

The first slight swerving of the heart,
    That words are powerless to express,
And leave it still unsaid in part,
    Or say it in too great excess.

        3 *

The **very** tones in which **we** spake
    Had something strange, I could **but mark**;
The leaves of memory seemed to **make**
    A mournful rustling in the dark.

Oft died the words upon our lips,
    As suddenly, from out the fire
Built of the wreck of stranded ships,
    The flames would leap and then expire.

And, as their splendor flashed and **failed,**
    We thought of wrecks upon the main, —
Of ships dismasted, that were hailed
    And **sent no answer** back again.

The windows, rattling in their frames, —
    The ocean, roaring up the beach, —
The gusty blast, — the bickering flames, —
    All mingled vaguely in our speech;

Until they made themselves a part
    Of fancies floating through the brain, —
The long-lost ventures of the heart,
    That **send** no answers **back** again.

O flames that glowed! O hearts that yearned!
    They were indeed too much akin,
The drift-wood fire without that burned,
    The thoughts that burned and glowed within.

RESIGNATION.

THERE is no flock, however watched and tended,
But one dead lamb is there!
There is no fireside, howsoe'er defended,
But has one vacant chair!

The air is full of farewells to the dying,
And mournings for the dead;
The heart of Rachel, for her children crying,
Will not be comforted!

Let us be patient! These severe afflictions
Not from the ground arise,
But oftentimes celestial benedictions
Assume this dark disguise.

We see but dimly through the mists and vapors;
Amid these earthly damps,
What seem to us but sad, funereal tapers
May be heaven's distant lamps.

There is no Death! What seems so is transition.
This life of mortal breath
Is but a suburb of the life elysian,
Whose portal we call Death.

She is not dead, — the child of our affection, —
But gone unto that school
Where she no longer needs our poor protection,
And Christ himself doth rule.

In that great cloister's stillness and seclusion,
By guardian angels led,
Safe from temptation, safe from sin's pollution,
She lives, whom we call dead.

Day after day we think what she is doing
   In those bright realms of air;
Year after year, her tender steps pursuing,
   Behold her grown more fair.

Thus do we walk with her, and keep unbroken
  The bond which nature gives,
Thinking that our remembrance, though unspoken,
  May reach her where she lives.

Not as a child shall we again behold **her**;
  For when with raptures wild
In our embraces we again enfold **her**,
  She will not be a child;

But a fair maiden, in her Father's **mansion**,
  Clothed with celestial grace;
And beautiful with all the soul's expansion
  Shall **we** behold her face.

And though at times impetuous with emotion
  And anguish long suppressed,
The swelling heart heaves moaning like the ocean,
  That cannot be at rest, —

We will be patient, and assuage the feeling
  We **may** not wholly stay;
By silence sanctifying, not concealing,
  The grief that must have way.

THE BUILDERS.

A LL are architects of Fate,
    Working in these walls of Time;
Some with massive deeds and great,
  Some with ornaments of rhyme.

Nothing useless is, or low;
  Each thing in its place is best;
And what seems but idle show
  Strengthens and supports the rest.

For the structure that we raise,
    Time is with materials filled ;
Our to-days and yesterdays
    Are the blocks with which we build.

Truly shape and fashion these ;
    Leave no yawning gaps between ;
Think not, because no man sees,
    Such things will remain unseen.

In the elder days of Art,
    Builders wrought with greatest care
Each minute and unseen part ;
    For the Gods see everywhere.

Let us do our work as well,
    Both the unseen and the seen ;
Make the house, where Gods may dwell,
    Beautiful, entire, and clean.

Else our lives are incomplete,
    Standing in these walls of Time,
Broken stairways,. where the feet
    Stumble as they seek to climb.

Build to-day, then, strong and sure,
    With a firm and ample base ;
And ascending and secure
    Shall to-morrow find its place.

Thus alone can we attain
    To those turrets, where the eye
Sees the world as one vast plain,
    And one boundless reach of sky.

THE OPEN WINDOW.

THE old house by the lindens
    Stood silent in the shade,
And on the gravelled pathway
    The light and shadow played.

I saw the nursery windows
    Wide open to the air ;
But the faces of the children,
    They were no longer there.

The large Newfoundland house-dog
  Was standing by the door;
He looked for his little playmates,
  Who would return no more.

They walked not under the lindens,
  They played not in the hall;
But shadow, and silence, and sadness
  Were hanging over all.

The birds sang in the branches,
  With sweet, familiar tone;
But the voices of the children
  Will be heard in dreams alone!

And the boy that walked beside me,
  He could not understand
Why closer in mine, ah! closer,
  I pressed his warm, soft hand!

SUSPIRIA.   .

TAKE them, O Death! and bear away
    Whatever thou canst call thine own!
Thine image, stamped upon this clay,
  Doth give thee that, but that alone!

Take them, O Grave! and let them lie
  Folded upon thy narrow shelves,
As garments by the soul laid by,
  And precious only to ourselves!

Take them, O great Eternity!
  Our little life is but a gust,
That bends the branches of thy tree,
  And trails its blossoms in the dust.

THE LADDER OF ST. AUGUSTINE.

S AINT AUGUSTINE! well hast thou said,
   That of our vices we can frame
A ladder, if we will but tread
   Beneath our feet each deed of shame!

        •

All common things, each day's events,
   That with the hour begin and end,
Our pleasures and our discontents,
   Are rounds by which we may ascend.

The low desire, the base design,
   That makes another's virtues less;
The revel of the ruddy wine,
   And all occasions of excess;

The longing for ignoble things;
   The strife for triumph more than truth;
The hardening of the heart, that brings
   Irreverence for the dreams of youth;

All thoughts of ill; all evil deeds,
   That have their root in thoughts of ill;
Whatever hinders or impedes
   The action of the nobler will; —

All these must first be trampled down
   Beneath our feet, if we would gain
In the bright fields of fair renown
   The right of eminent domain.

We have not wings, we cannot soar;
   But we have feet to scale and climb
By slow degrees, by more and more,
   The cloudy summits of our time.

The mighty pyramids of stone
    That wedge-like cleave the desert airs,
When nearer seen, and better known,
    Are but gigantic flights of stairs.

The distant mountains, that uprear
    Their solid bastions to the skies,
Are crossed by pathways, that appear
    As we to higher levels rise.

The heights by great men reached and kept,
    Were not attained by sudden flight,
But they, while their companions slept,
    Were toiling upward in the night.

Standing on what too long we bore
    With shoulders bent and downcast eyes,
We may discern — unseen before —
    A path to higher destinies.

Nor deem the irrevocable Past,
    As wholly wasted, wholly vain,
If, rising on its wrecks, at last
    To something nobler we attain.

HAUNTED HOUSES.

ALL houses wherein men have lived and died
    Are haunted houses. Through the open doors
The harmless phantoms on their errands glide,
    With feet that make no sound upon the floors.

We meet them at the door-way, on the stair,
    Along the passages they come and go,
Impalpable impressions on the air,
    A sense of something moving to and fro.

There are more guests at table, than the hosts
  Invited; the illuminated hall
Is thronged with quiet, inoffensive ghosts,
  As silent as the pictures on the wall.

The stranger at my fireside cannot see
  The forms I see, nor hear the sounds I hear;
He but perceives what is; while unto me
  All that has been is visible and clear.

We have no title-deeds to house or lands;
  Owners and occupants of earlier dates
From graves forgotten stretch their dusty hands,
  And hold in mortmain still their old estates.

The spirit-world around this world of sense
  Floats like an atmosphere, and everywhere
Wafts through these earthly mists and vapors dense
  A vital breath of more ethereal air.

Our little lives are kept in equipoise
  By opposite attractions and desires;
The struggle of the instinct that enjoys,
  And the more noble instinct that aspires.

These perturbations, this perpetual jar
  Of earthly wants and aspirations high,
Come from the influence of an unseen star,
  An undiscovered planet in our sky.

And as the moon from some dark gate of cloud
  Throws o'er the sea a floating bridge of light,
Across whose trembling planks our fancies crowd
  Into the realm of mystery and night, —

So from the world of spirits there descends
  A bridge of light, connecting it with this,
O'er whose unsteady floor, that sways and bends,
  Wander our thoughts above the dark abyss.

IN THE CHURCHYARD AT CAMBRIDGE.

IN the village churchyard she lies,
   Dust is in her beautiful eyes,
  No more she breathes, nor feels, nor stirs;
At her feet and at her head
Lies a slave to attend the dead,
  But their dust is white as hers.

Was she a lady of high degree,
So much in love with the vanity
  And foolish pomp of this world of ours?
Or was it Christian charity,
And lowliness and humility,
  The richest and rarest of all dowers?

Who shall tell us? No one speaks;
No color shoots into those cheeks,
  Either of anger or of pride,
At the rude question we have asked;
Nor will the mystery be unmasked
  By those who are sleeping at her side.

Hereafter? — And do you think to look
On the terrible pages of that Book
  To find her failings, faults, and errors?
Ah, you will then have other cares,
In your own short-comings and despairs,
  In your own secret sins and terrors!

THE TWO ANGELS.

TWO angels, one of Life and one of Death,
  Passed o'er our village as the morning broke;
The dawn was on their faces, and beneath,
  The sombre houses hearsed with plumes of smoke.

Their attitude and aspect were the same,
  Alike their features and their robes of white;
But one was crowned with amaranth, as with flame,
  And one with asphodels, like flakes of light.

I saw them pause on their celestial way;
  Then said I, with deep fear and doubt oppressed,
"Beat not so loud, my heart, lest thou betray
  The place where thy beloved are at rest!"

And he who wore the crown of asphodels,
  Descending, at my door began to knock,
And my soul sank within me, as in wells
  The waters sink before an earthquake's shock.

I recognized the nameless agony,
  The terror and the tremor and the pain,
That oft before had filled or haunted me,
  And now returned with threefold strength again.

The door I opened to my heavenly guest,
  And listened, for I thought I heard God's voice;
And, knowing whatsoe'er he sent was best,
  Dared neither to lament nor to rejoice.

Then with a smile, that filled the house with light,
  "My errand is not Death, but Life," he said;
And ere I answered, passing out of sight,
  On his celestial embassy he sped.

'T was at thy door, O friend! and not at mine,
  The angel with the amaranthine wreath,
Pausing, descended, and with voice divine,
  Whispered a word that had a sound like Death.

Then fell upon the house a sudden gloom,
  A shadow on those features fair and thin;
And softly, from that hushed and darkened room,
  Two angels issued, where but one went in.

All is of God! If he but wave his hand,
  The mists collect, the rain falls thick and loud,
Till, with a smile of light on sea and land,
  Lo! he looks back from the departing cloud.

Angels of Life and Death alike are his;
  Without his leave they pass no threshold o'er;
Who, then, would wish or dare, believing this,
  Against his messengers to shut the door?

DAYLIGHT AND MOONLIGHT.

I N broad daylight, and at noon,
  Yesterday I saw the moon
Sailing high, but faint and white,
As a schoolboy's paper kite.

In broad daylight, yesterday,
I read a Poet's mystic lay;
And it seemed to me at most
As a phantom, or a ghost.

But at length the feverish **day**
Like a passion died away,
And the night, serene and still,
Fell on village, vale, and hill.

Then the moon, in all her pride,
Like a spirit glorified,
Filled and overflowed the night
With revelations of her light.

And the Poet's song again
Passed like music through my **brain**;
Night interpreted to me
All its grace and mystery.

MY LOST YOUTH.

O FTEN I think of the beautiful **town**
  That is seated by the sea;
Often in thought go up and down
The pleasant streets of that dear old **town**,
  And my youth comes back to me.

And a verse of a Lapland song
Is haunting my memory still :
" A boy's will is the wind's will,
And the thoughts of youth are long, long thoughts."

I can see the shadowy lines of its trees,
    And catch, in sudden gleams,
The sheen of the far-surrounding seas,
And islands that were the Hesperides
    Of all my boyish dreams.
        And the burden of that old song,
        It murmurs and whispers still :
    " A boy's will is the wind's will,
And the thoughts of youth are long, long thoughts."

I remember the black wharves and the slips,
    And the sea-tides tossing free ;
And Spanish sailors with bearded lips,
And the beauty and mystery of the ships,
    And the magic of the sea.
        And the voice of that wayward song
        Is singing and saying still :
    " A boy's will is the wind's will,
And the thoughts of youth are long, long thoughts."

I remember the bulwarks by the shore,
    And the fort upon the hill ;
The sun-rise gun, with its hollow roar,
The drum-beat repeated o'er and o'er,
    And the bugle wild and shrill.
        And the music of that old song
        Throbs in my memory still :
    " A boy's will is the wind's will,
And the thoughts of youth are long, long thoughts."

I remember the sea-fight far away,
    How it thundered o'er the tide !
And the dead captains, as they lay
In their graves, o'erlooking the tranquil bay,
    Where they in battle died.

And the sound of that mournful song
  Goes through me with a thrill :
"**A** boy's will is the wind's will,
And the thoughts of youth are long, long thoughts."

I can see the breezy dome of groves,
  The shadows of Deering's Woods ;
And the friendships old and the early loves
Came back with a Sabbath sound, as of doves
  In quiet neighborhoods.
    And the verse of that sweet old song,
    It flutters and murmurs still :
"A boy's will is the wind's will,
And the thoughts of youth are long, long thoughts."

I remember the gleams and glooms that dart
  Across the schoolboy's brain ;
The song and the silence in the heart,
That in part are prophecies, **and in part**
  Are longings wild and vain.
    And the voice of that fitful song
    Sings on, and is never still :
"**A** boy's will is the wind's will,
And the thoughts of **youth** are long, long thoughts."

There are things of which I may not speak ;
  There **are** dreams that cannot die ;
There are thoughts that make **the strong heart weak,**
And bring a pallor into the cheek,
  And a **mist** before the eye.
    And the **words of** that fatal song
    Come over me like a chill :
"A boy's **will is the** wind's will,
And the thoughts of youth are long, long thoughts."

Strange to me now are the forms I meet
  When I visit the dear old town ;
But the native air is pure and sweet,
And the trees that o'ershadow each well-known **street,**
  As they balance up and down,

4

Are singing the beautiful song,
Are sighing and whispering still :
" A boy's will is the wind's will,
And the thoughts of youth are long, long thoughts."

And Deering's Woods are fresh and fair,
And with joy that is almost pain
My heart goes back to wander there,
And among the dreams of the days that were,
I find my lost youth again.
And the strange and beautiful song,
The groves are repeating it still :
" A boy's will is the wind's will,
And the thoughts of youth are long, long thoughts."

THE GOLDEN MILESTONE.

LEAFLESS are the trees ; their purple branches
Spread themselves abroad, like reefs of coral,
Rising silent
In the Red Sea of the Winter sunset.

From the hundred chimneys of the village,
Like the Afreet in the Arabian story,
Smoky columns
Tower aloft into the air of amber.

At the window winks the flickering fire-light ;
Here and there the lamps of evening glimmer,
Social watch-fires
Answering one another through the darkness.

On the hearth the lighted logs are glowing,
And like Ariel in the cloven pine-tree
For its freedom
Groans and sighs the air imprisoned in them.

By the fireside there are old men seated,
Seeing ruined cities in the ashes,
   Asking sadly
Of the Past what it can ne'er restore them.

By the fireside there are youthful dreamers,
Building castles fair, with stately stairways,
   Asking blindly
Of the Future what it cannot give them.

By the fireside tragedies are acted
In whose scenes appear two actors only,
   Wife and husband,
And above them God the sole spectator.

By the fireside there are peace and comfort,
Wives and children, with fair, thoughtful faces,
   Waiting, watching
For a well-known footstep in the passage.

Each man's chimney is his Golden Mile-stone;
Is the central point, from which he measures
   Every distance
Through the gateways of the world around him.

In his farthest wanderings still he sees it ;
Hears the talking flame, the answering night-wind,
   As he heard them
When he sat with those who were, but are not

Happy he whom neither wealth nor fashion,
Nor the march of the encroaching city,
   Drives an exile
From the hearth of his ancestral homestead.

We may build more splendid habitations,
Fill our rooms with paintings and with sculptures,
   But we cannot
Buy with gold the old associations !

DAYBREAK.

A WIND came up out of the sea,
And said, "O mists, make room for me."

It hailed the ships, and cried, " Sail on,
Ye mariners, the night is gone."

And hurried landward far away,
Crying, "Awake! it is the day."

It said unto the forest, " Shout!
Hang all your leafy banners out!"

It touched the wood-bird's folded wing,
And said, "O bird, awake and sing."

And o'er the farms, " O chanticleer,
Your clarion blow; the day is near."

It whispered to the fields of corn,
" Bow down, and hail the coming morn."

It shouted through the belfry-tower,
"Awake, O bell! proclaim the hour."

It crossed the churchyard with a sigh,
And said, "Not yet! in quiet lie."

THE ROPEWALK.

I N that building, long and low,
With its windows all a-row,
Like the port-holes of a hulk,
Human spiders spin and spin,
Backward down their threads so thin
Dropping, each a hempen bulk.

At the end, an open door;
Squares of sunshine on the floor
Light the long and dusky lane;

And the whirring of a wheel,
Dull and drowsy, makes me feel
   All its spokes are in my brain.

As the spinners to the end
Downward go and reascend,
   Gleam the long threads in the **sun**;
While within this brain of mine
Cobwebs brighter and more fine
   By the busy wheel are spun.

Two fair maidens **in a** swing,
Like white doves **upon** the wing,
   First before my **vision** pass;
Laughing, as their **gentle** hands
Closely clasp the **twisted** strands,
   At their shadow **on** the grass.

Then a booth of mountebanks,
With its smell of tan and planks,
   And a girl poised high in air
On a cord, in spangled dress,
With a faded loveliness,
   And a weary look of care.

Then a homestead among farms,
And a woman with **bare** arms
   Drawing water **from a well**;
As the bucket mounts apace,
With it mounts her own fair face,
   As at some magician's spell.

Then an old man in a tower,
Ringing loud the noontide hour,
   While the rope coils round and round
Like **a** serpent at his feet,
And again, in swift retreat,
   Nearly lifts him from the ground.

Then within a prison-yard,
Faces fixed, and stern, and hard,
  Laughter and indecent mirth ;
Ah ! it is the gallows-tree !
Breath of Christian charity,
  Blow, and sweep it from the earth !

Then a school-boy, with his kite
Gleaming in a sky of light,
  And an eager, upward look ;
Steeds pursued through **lane** and field ;
Fowlers with their snares concealed ;
  And an angler by a brook.

Ships rejoicing in the breeze,
Wrecks that float o'er unknown seas,
  Anchors dragged through faithless sand ;
Sea-fog drifting overhead,
And, with lessening line and lead,
  Sailors feeling for the land.

All these scenes **do I** behold,
These, and many **left** untold,
  In that building long and low ;
While the wheel goes round and round,
With **a** drowsy, dreamy sound,
  And the spinners backward go.

SANDALPHON.

HAVE you read in the Talmud of old,
    In the Legends the Rabbins have told
  Of the limitless realms of the air, —
Have you, read it, — the marvellous story
Of Sandalphon, the Angel of Glory,.
  Sandalphon, the Angel of Prayer ?

How, erect, at the outermost gates
Of the City Celestial he waits,
    With his feet on the ladder **of light,**
That, crowded **with** angels unnumbered,
By Jacob was seen, as he slumbered
    Alone in the desert at night?

The Angels of Wind and of Fire
Chaunt only one hymn, and expire
    With the song's irresistible stress;
Expire in their rapture and wonder,
As harp-strings are broken asunder
    By music they throb to express.

But serene in the rapturous **throng,**
Unmoved by the rush of the song,
    With eyes unimpassioned and slow,
Among the dead angels, the deathless
Sandalphon stands listening breathless
    To sounds that ascend from below;—

From the spirits on earth **that adore,**
From the souls that entreat and **implore**
    In the fervor and passion of prayer;
From the hearts that are broken with losses,
And weary with dragging **the** crosses
    Too heavy for mortals to bear.

And he gathers the prayers as he stands,
And they change into flowers **in** his hands,
    Into garlands of purple and red;
And beneath **the** great arch of the portal,
Through the streets of the City Immortal
    Is wafted the fragrance they shed.

It is but a legend, I know,—
A fable, **a phantom,** a show,
    Of the ancient Rabbinical **lore;**
Yet the old mediæval tradition,
The beautiful, strange superstition,
    But haunts me and holds me the more.

When I look from my window at night,
And the welkin above is all white,
  All throbbing and panting with stars,
Among them majestic is standing
Sandalphon the angel, expanding
  His pinions in nebulous bars.

And the legend, I feel, is a part
Of the hunger and thirst of the heart,
  The frenzy and fire of the brain,
That grasps at the fruitage forbidden,
The golden pomegranates of Eden,
  To quiet its fever and pain.

THE CHILDREN'S HOUR.

BETWEEN the dark and the daylight,
  When the night is beginning to lower,
Comes a pause in the day's occupations,
  That is known as the Children's Hour.

I hear in the chamber above me
  The patter of little feet,
The sound of a door that is opened,
  And voices soft and sweet.

From my study I see in the lamplight,
  Descending the broad hall stair,
Grave Alice, and laughing Allegra,
  And Edith with golden hair.

A whisper, and then a silence:
  Yet I know by their merry eyes
They are plotting and planning together
  To take me by surprise.

4 *   F

A sudden rush from the stairway,
　A sudden raid from the hall!
By three doors left unguarded
　They enter my castle wall!

They climb up into my turret
　O'er the arms and back of my chair;
If I try to escape, they surround me;
　They seem to be everywhere.

They almost devour me with kisses,
　Their arms about me entwine,
Till I think of the Bishop of Bingen
　In his Mouse-Tower on the Rhine!

Do you think, O blue-eyed banditti,
　Because you have scaled the wall,
Such an old moustache as I am
　Is not a match for you all!

I have you fast in my fortress,
　And will not let you depart,
But put you down into the dungeon
　In the round-tower of my heart.

And there will I keep you forever,
　Yes, forever and a day,
Till the walls shall crumble to ruin,
　And moulder in dust away!

SNOW-FLAKES.

OUT of the bosom of the Air,
　Out of the cloud-folds of her garments shaken,
Over the woodlands brown and bare,
　Over the harvest-fields forsaken,
　　Silent, and soft, and slow
　　Descends the snow.

Even as our cloudy fancies take
  Suddenly shape in some divine expression,
Even ás the troubled heart doth make
  In the white countenance confession,
     The troubled sky **reveals**
     The grief it feels.

This is the poem of the air,
  Slowly in silent syllables recorded ;
This is the secret of despair,
  Long in its cloudy bosom hoarded,
     Now whispered and revealed
     To wood and field.

A DAY OF SUNSHINE.

O GIFT of God! O perfect day :
    Whereon shall no man work, but play ;
Whereon it is enough for me,
Not to be doing, but to be !

Through every fibre of my brain,
Through every nerve, through every vein,
I feel the electric thrill, the touch
Of life, that seems almost too **much.**

I hear the wind among the trees
Playing celestial symphonies ;
 · I see the branches downward bent,
Like keys of some great instrument.

And over me unrolls **on** high
The splendid scenery of the sky,
Where through a sapphire sea the sun
Sails **like** a golden galleon,

Towards yonder cloud-land in the West,
Towards yonder Islands of the Blest,
Whose steep sierra far uplifts
Its craggy summits white with drifts.

Blow, winds! and waft through all the rooms
The snow-flakes of the cherry-blooms!
Blow, winds! and bend within my reach
The fiery blossoms of the peach!

O Life and Love! O happy throng
Of thoughts, whose only speech is song!
O heart of man! canst thou not be
Blithe as the air is, and as free?

SOMETHING LEFT UNDONE.

LABOR with what zeal we will,
    Something still remains undone,
Something uncompleted still
    Waits the rising of the sun.

By the bedside, on the stair,
    At the threshold, near the gates,
With its menace or its prayer,
    Like a mendicant it waits;

Waits, and will not go away;
    Waits, and will not be gainsaid;
By the cares of yesterday
    Each to-day is heavier made;

Till at length the burden seems
    Greater than our strength can bear,
Heavy as the weight of dreams,
    Pressing on us everywhere.

And we stand from day to day,
  Like the dwarfs of times gone **by,**
Who, as Northern legends say,
  On their shoulders held the sky.

WEARINESS.

O LITTLE feet! that such long years
  Must wander on through hopes and fears,
Must ache and bleed beneath your load;
I, nearer to the wayside **inn**
Where toil shall cease and rest begin,
  Am weary, thinking of your road!

O little hands! that, **weak or strong,**
Have still **to serve or rule so** long,
  Have still so long to give or ask;
I, who so much with book and pen
Have toiled among my fellow-men,
  Am weary, thinking of your task.

O little hearts! that throb and beat
With such impatient, feverish heat,
  Such limitless and strong desires;
Mine that so long has glowed and burned,
With passions into ashes turned
  Now covers and conceals its fires.

O little souls! as pure and white
And crystalline as rays **of** light
  Direct from heaven, their source divine;
Refracted through the mist of years,
How red my setting sun appears,
  How lurid looks this soul **of mine!**

CHILDREN.

COME to me, O ye children!
   For I hear you at your play,
And the questions that perplexed me
   Have vanished quite away.

Ye open the eastern windows,
  That look towards the sun,
Where thoughts are singing swallows
  And the brooks of morning run.

In your hearts are the birds and the sunshine,
  In your thoughts the brooklet's flow,
But in mine is the wind of Autumn
  And the first fall of the snow.

Ah! what would the world be to us
  If the children were no more?
We should dread the desert behind us
  Worse than the dark before.

What the leaves are to the forest,
  With light and air for food,
Ere their sweet and tender juices
  Have been hardened into wood, —

That to the world are children;
  Through them it feels the glow
Of a brighter and sunnier climate
  Than reaches the trunks below.

Come to me, O ye children!
  And whisper in my ear
What the birds and the winds are singing
  In your sunny atmosphere.

For what are all our contrivings,
  And the wisdom of our books,
When compared with your caresses,
  And the gladness of your looks?

Ye are better than all the ballads
  That ever were sung or said;
For ye are living poems,
  And all the rest are dead.

THE BRIDGE OF CLOUD.

BURN, O evening hearth, and waken
    Pleasant visions, as of old!
Though the house by winds be shaken,
    Safe I keep this room of gold!

Ah! no longer wizard Fancy
    Builds its castles in the air,
Luring me by necromancy
    Up the never-ending stair.

But, instead, it builds me bridges
    Over many a dark ravine,
Where beneath the gusty ridges
    Cataracts dash and roar unseen.

And I cross them, little heeding
    Blast of wind or torrent's roar,
As I follow the receding
    Footsteps that have gone before.

Naught avails the imploring gesture,
    Naught avails the cry of pain!
When I touch the flying vesture,
    'T is the gray robe of the rain.

Baffled I return, and, leaning
    O'er the parapets of cloud,
Watch the mist that intervening
    Wraps the valley in its shroud.

And the sounds of life ascending
    Faintly, vaguely, meet the ear,
Murmur of bells and voices blending
    With the rush of waters near.

Well I know what there lies hidden,
    Every tower and town and farm,
And again the land forbidden
    Reassumes its vanished charm.

Well I know the secret places,
    And the nests in hedge and tree;
At what doors are friendly faces,
    In what hearts a thought of me.

Through the mist and darkness sinking,
    Blown by wind and beaten by shower,
Down I fling the thought I 'm thinking,
    Down I toss this Alpine flower.

PALINGENESIS.

I LAY upon the headland-height, and listened
    To the incessant sobbing of the sea
        In caverns under me,
And watched the waves, that tossed and fled and glistened,
Until the rolling meadows of amethyst
        Melted away in mist.

Then suddenly, as one from sleep, I started;
For round about me all the sunny capes
        Seemed peopled with the shapes
Of those whom I had known in days departed,
Apparelled in the loveliness which gleams
        On faces seen in dreams.

A moment only, and the light and glory
Faded away, and the disconsolate shore
        Stood lonely as before;
And the wild roses of the promontory
Around me shuddered in the wind, and shed
        Their petals of pale red.

There was an old belief that in the embers
Of all things their primordial form exists,
    And cunning alchemists
Could recreate the rose with all its members
From its own ashes, but without the bloom,
    Without the lost perfume.

Ah me! what wonder-working, occult science
Can from the ashes in our hearts once more
    The rose of youth restore?
What craft of alchemy can bid defiance
To time and change, and for a single hour
    Renew this phantom-flower?

"O, give me back," I cried, "the vanished splendors,
The breath of morn, and the exultant strife,
    When the swift stream of life
Bounds o'er its rocky channel, and surrenders
The pond, with all its lilies, for the leap
    Into the unknown deep!"

And the sea answered, with a lamentation,
Like some old prophet wailing, and it said,
    "Alas! thy youth is dead!
It breathes no more, its heart has no pulsation,
In the dark places with the dead of old
    It lies forever cold!"

Then said I, "From its consecrated cerements
I will not drag this sacred dust again,
    Only to give me pain;
But, still remembering all the lost endearments,
Go on my way, like one who looks before,
    And turns to weep no more."

Into what land of harvests, what plantations
Bright with autumnal foliage and the glow
    Of sunsets burning low;

Beneath what midnight skies, whose constellations
Light up the spacious avenues between
    This world and the unseen!

Amid what friendly greetings and caresses,
What households, though not alien, yet not **mine**,
    What bowers of rest divine;
To what temptations in lone wildernesses,
What famine of the heart, what pain and loss,
    The bearing **of what cross**

I do not know; nor will I vainly question
Those pages **of** the mystic book which hold
    The story still untold,
But without rash conjecture or suggestion
Turn its last leaves in reverence and good heed,
    Until "The End" I read.

THE BROOK.

FROM THE SPANISH.

LAUGH of the mountain! — lyre of bird and tree!
    Pomp of the meadow! mirror of the morn!
The soul of April, unto whom are born
The rose **and** jessamine, leaps wild in thee!
Although, where'er thy devious current strays,
The lap of earth with gold and silver teems,
To me thy clear proceeding **brighter** seems
Than golden sands, that charm each shepherd's gaze.
How without guile thy bosom, all transparent
As the pure crystal, lets the curious **eye**
Thy secrets scan, thy smooth, round pebbles **count!**
How, without malice murmuring, glides thy current!
O sweet simplicity of days gone by!
.**Thou** shun'st the haunts of man, to dwell in limpid **fount!**

SONG OF THE SILENT LAND.

FROM THE GERMAN OF SALIS.

INTO the Silent Land!
Ah! who shall lead us thither?
Clouds in the evening sky more darkly gather,
And shattered wrecks lie thicker on the strand.
Who leads us with a gentle hand
Thither, O thither,
Into the Silent Land?

Into the Silent Land!
To you, ye boundless regions
Of all perfection! Tender morning visions
Of beauteous souls! The Future's pledge and band
Who in Life's battle firm doth stand,
Shall bear Hope's tender blossoms
Into the Silent Land!

O Land! O Land!
For all the broken-hearted
The mildest herald by our fate allotted,
Beckons, and with inverted torch doth stand
To lead us with a gentle hand
Into the land of the great Departed,
Into the Silent Land!

THE TWO LOCKS OF HAIR.

FROM THE GERMAN OF PFIZER.

A YOUTH, light-hearted and content,
  I wander through **the** world;
Here, Arab-like, is pitched my tent
  And straight again **is furled.**

Yet oft I dream, **that once a wife**
  Close in my heart was locked,
And in the sweet repose of life
  A blessed child I rocked.

I wake! Away that dream, — away!
  Too long did it remain!
So long, that both by night and **day**
  It **ever** comes **again.**

The end lies ever in my thought;   •
  To a grave so cold and deep
The mother beautiful was brought;
  Then dropt the child asleep.

But now the dream is wholly o'er,
  I bathe mine eyes and see;
And wander through the world once more,
  A youth so light **and** free.

Two locks, — and they are wondrous fair, —
  Left me that **vision mild;**
The brown is from **the mother's hair,**
  The blond is from the child.

And when I see that lock **of gold,**
  Pale grows the evening-red;
And when the dark lock I behold,
  I wish that I were dead.

THE SINGERS.

GOD sent his Singers upon earth
With songs of sadness and of mirth,
That they might touch the hearts of men,
And bring them back to heaven again.

The first, a youth, with soul of fire,
Held in his hand a golden lyre;
Through groves he wandered, and by streams,
Playing the music of our dreams.

The second, with a bearded face,
Stood singing in the market-place,
And stirred with accents deep and loud
The hearts of all the listening crowd.

A gray, old man, the third and last,
Sang in cathedrals dim and vast,
While the majestic organ rolled
Contrition from its mouths of gold.

And those who heard the Singers three
Disputed which the best might be;
For still their music seemed to start
Discordant echoes in each heart.

But the great Master said, "I see
No best in kind, but in degree;
I gave a various gift to each,
To charm, to strengthen, and to teach.

"These are the three great chords of might,
And he whose ear is tuned aright
Will hear no discord in the three,
But the most perfect harmony."

CHRISTMAS BELLS.

I HEARD the bells on Christmas Day
Their old, familiar carols play,
    And wild and sweet
    The words repeat
Of peace on earth, good-will to men!

And thought how, as the day had come,
The belfries of all Christendom
    Had rolled along
    The unbroken song
Of peace on earth, good-will to men!

Till, ringing, singing on its way,
The world revolved from night to day,
    A voice, a chime,
    A chant sublime
Of peace on earth, good-will to men!

Then from each black, accursed mouth,
The cannon thundered in the South,
    And with the sound
    The carols drowned
Of peace on earth, good-will to men!

It was as if an earthquake rent
The hearth-stones of a continent,
    And made forlorn
    The households born
Of peace on earth, good-will to men!

And in despair I bowed my head;
"There is no peace on earth," I said;
    "For hate is strong
    And mocks the song
Of peace on earth, good-will to men!"

Then pealed the bells more loud and deep :
" God is not dead ; nor doth he sleep !
  The Wrong shall fail,
  The Right prevail,
With peace on earth, good-will to men ! "

Cambridge : Electrotyped and Printed by Welch, Bigelow, & Co.

SONGS FOR ALL SEASONS.

BY

ALFRED TENNYSON.

With Illustrations by

D. MACLISE, T. CRESWICK, S. EYTINGE, C. A. BARRY,
H. FENN, AND G. PERKINS.

BOSTON:
JAMES R. OSGOOD AND COMPANY,
LATE TICKNOR & FIELDS, AND FIELDS, OSGOOD, & CO.
1871.

"It is my wish that with MESSRS. TICKNOR AND FIELDS alone the right of publishing my books in America should rest."

ALFRED TENNYSON.

UNIVERSITY PRESS:
WELCH, BIGELOW, AND COMPANY,
CAMBRIDGE.

CONTENTS.

CONTENTS.

SONGS FOR ALL SEASONS.

COME INTO THE GARDEN, MAUD.

COME into the garden, Maud,
    For the black bat, night, has flown;
Come into the garden, Maud,
    I am here at the gate alone;
And the woodbine spices are wafted abroad,
    And the musk of the roses blown.

For a breeze of morning moves,
    And the planet of Love is on high,
Beginning to faint in the light that she loves
    On a bed of daffodil sky, —
To faint in the light of the sun she loves,
    To faint in his light, and to die.

All night have the roses heard
    The flute, violin, bassoon;
All night has the casement jessamine stirr'd
    To the dancers dancing in tune:
Till a silence fell with the waking bird,
    And a hush with the setting moon.

I said to the lily, "There is but one
    With whom she has heart to be gay.
When will the dancers leave her alone?
    She is weary of dance and play."
Now half to the setting moon are gone,
    And half to the rising day;
Low on the sand and loud on the stone
    The last wheel echoes away.

I said to the rose, "The brief night goes
    In babble and revel and wine.
O young lord-lover, what sighs are those,
    For one that will never be thine?
But mine, but mine," so I sware to the rose,
    "For ever and ever, mine."

And the soul of the rose went into my blood,
    As the music clash'd in the hall;
And long by the garden lake I stood,
    For I heard your rivulet fall
From the lake to the meadow and on to the wood,
    Our wood, that is dearer than all;

From the meadow your walks have left so sweet
    That whenever a March-wind sighs
He sets the jewel-print of your feet
    In violets blue as your eyes,
To the woody hollows in which we meet
    And the valleys of Paradise.

The slender acacia would not shake
    One long milk-bloom on the tree;
The white lake-blossom fell into the lake,
    As the pimpernel dozed on the lea;

But the rose was awake all night for your sake,
  Knowing your promise to me ;
The lilies and roses were all awake,
  They sigh'd for the dawn and thee.

Queen rose of the rosebud garden of girls,
  Come hither, the dances are done,
In gloss of satin and glimmer of pearls,
  Queen lily and rose in one ;
Shine out, little head, sunning over with curls
  To the flowers, and be their sun.

There has fallen a splendid tear
  From the passion-flower at the gate.
She is coming, my dove, my dear;
  She is coming, my life, my fate;
The red rose cries, " She is near, she is near";
  And the white rose weeps, " She is late";
The larkspur listens, " I hear, I hear ";
  And the lily whispers, " I wait."

She is coming, my own, my sweet;
  Were it ever so airy a tread,
My heart would hear her and beat,
  Were it earth in an earthy bed;
My dust would hear her and beat,
  Had I lain for a century dead;
Would start and tremble under her feet,
  And blossom in purple and red.

A VOICE BY THE CEDAR-TREE.

A VOICE by the cedar-tree,
  In the meadow under the Hall!
She is singing an air that is known to me,
A passionate ballad, gallant and gay,
A martial song like a trumpet's call!
Singing alone in the morning of life,
In the happy morning of life and of May,
Singing of men that in battle array,
Ready in heart and ready in hand,
March with banner and bugle and fife
To the death, for their native land.

Maud with her exquisite face,
And wild voice pealing up to the sunny sky,
And feet like sunny gems on an English green,
Maud in the light of her youth and her grace,
Singing of Death, and of Honor that cannot die,
Till I well could weep for a time so sordid and mean
And myself so languid and base.

Silence, beautiful voice!
Be still, for you only trouble the mind
With a joy in which I cannot rejoice,
A glory I shall not find.
Still! I will hear you no more,
For your sweetness hardly leaves me a choice
But to move to the meadow and fall before
Her feet on the meadow grass, and adore,
Not her, who is neither courtly nor kind,
Not her, not her, but a voice.

O LET THE SOLID GROUND.

O LET the solid ground
   Not fail beneath my feet
Before my life has found
   What some have found so sweet.
Then let come what come may,
What matter if I go mad,
I shall have had my day.

Let the sweet heavens endure,
   Not close and darken above me

Before I am quite quite sure
   That there is one to love me;
Then let come what come may
To a life that has been so sad,
I shall have had my day.

ı

BIRDS IN THE HIGH HALL-GARDEN.

BIRDS in the high Hall-garden
   When twilight was falling,
Maud, Maud, Maud, Maud,
   They were crying and calling.

Where was Maud? in our wood;
   And I, who else, was with her,
Gathering woodland lilies,
   Myriads blow together.

Birds in our wood sang
   Ringing thro' the valleys,
Maud is here, here, here
   In among the lilies.

I kissed her slender hand,
   She took the kiss sedately;
Maud is not seventeen,
   But she is tall and stately.

I to cry out on pride
   Who have won her favor!
O Maud were sure of Heaven
   If lowliness could save her.

I know the way she went
    Home with her maiden posy,
For her feet have touch'd the meadows
    And left the daisies rosy.

Birds in the high Hall-garden
    Were crying and calling to her,
Where is Maud, Maud, Maud,
    One is come to woo her.

Look, a horse at the door,
    And little King Charles is snarling.
Go back, my lord, across the moor,
    You are not her darling.

GO NOT, HAPPY DAY.

GO not, happy day,
    From the shining fields,
Go not, happy day,
Till the maiden yields.
Rosy is the West,
Rosy is the South,
Roses are her cheeks,
And a rose her mouth.
When the happy Yes
Falters from her lips,
Pass and blush the news
O'er the blowing ships.

Over blowing seas,
Over seas at rest,
Pass the happy news,
Blush it thro' the West;
Till the red man dance
By his red cedar-tree,
And the red man's babe
Leap, beyond the sea.
Blush from West to East,
Blush from East to West,
Till the West is East,
Blush it thro' the West.
Rosy is the West,
Rosy is the South,
Roses are her cheeks,
And a rose her mouth.

THE BUGLE SONG.

THE splendor falls on castle walls
    And snowy summits old in story;
The long light shakes across the lakes,
    And the wild cataract leaps in glory.
Blow, bugle, blow, set the wild echoes flying
Blow, bugle; answer, echoes, dying, dying, dying.

O hark, O hear! how thin and clear,
    And thinner, clearer, farther going;

O sweet and far, from cliff and scar,
    The horns of Elfland faintly blowing!
Blow, let us hear the purple glens replying:
Blow, bugle; answer, echoes, dying, dying, dying.

O love, they die in yon rich sky,
    They faint on hill or field or river:
Our echoes roll from soul to soul,
    And grow forever and forever.
Blow, bugle, blow, set the wild echoes flying,
And answer, echoes, answer, dying, dying, dying.

TEARS, IDLE TEARS.

TEARS, idle tears, I know not what they mean,
   Tears from the depth of some divine despair
Rise in the heart, and gather to the eyes,
In looking on the happy Autumn-fields,
And thinking of the days that are no more.

   Fresh as the first beam glittering on a sail,
That brings our friends up from the underworld,
Sad as the last which reddens over one
That sinks with all we love below the verge;
So sad, so fresh, the days that are no more.

   Ah, sad and strange as in dark summer dawns
The earliest pipe of half-awakened birds
To dying ears, when unto dying eyes
The casement slowly glows a glimmering square;
So sad, so strange, the days that are no more.

   Dear as remembered kisses after death,
And sweet as those by hopeless fancy feigned
On lips that are for others; deep as love,
Deep as first love, and wild with all regret,
O Death in Life, the days that are no more.

SONG TO THE SWALLOW.

O SWALLOW, Swallow, flying South,
  Fly to her, and fall upon her gilded eaves,
And tell her, tell her what I tell to thee.

  O tell her, Swallow, thou that knowest each,
That bright and fierce and fickle is the South,
And dark and true and tender is the North.

  O Swallow, Swallow, if I could follow, and light
Upon her lattice, I would pipe and trill,
And cheep and twitter twenty million loves.

  O were I thou that she might take me in,
And lay me on her bosom, and her heart
Would rock the snowy cradle till I died.

  Why lingereth she to clothe her heart with love,
Delaying as the tender ash delays
To clothe herself, when all the woods are green?

  O tell her, Swallow, that thy brood is flown:
Say to her, I do but wanton in the South,
But in the North long since my nest is made.

  O tell her, brief is life but love is long,
And brief the sun of summer in the North,
And brief the moon of beauty in the South.

  O Swallow, flying from the golden woods,
Fly to her, and pipe and woo her, and make her mine,
And tell her, tell her, that I follow thee."

ENID'S SONG.

TURN, Fortune, turn thy wheel and lower the proud;
   Turn thy wild wheel thro' sunshine, storm, and cloud;
Thy wheel and thee we neither love nor hate.

   Turn, Fortune, turn thy wheel with smile or frown;
With that wild wheel we go not up or down;
Our hoard is little, but our hearts are great.

   Smile and we smile, the lords of many lands;
Frown and we smile, the lords of our own hands;
For man is man and master of his fate.

   Turn, turn thy wheel above the staring crowd;
Thy wheel and thou are shadows in the cloud;
Thy wheel and thee we neither love nor hate.

VIVIEN'S SONG.

IN Love, if Love be Love, if Love be ours,
   Faith and unfaith can ne'er be equal powers;
Unfaith in aught is want of faith in all.

   It is the little rift within the lute
That by and by will make the music mute,
And ever widening slowly silence all.

The little rift within the **lover's lute,**
Or little pitted speck in garner'd fruit,
That rotting inward slowly moulders all.

It is not worth the keeping : let it go :
But shall it? answer, darling, answer, no.
And trust me not at all or all in all.

ELAINE'S SONG.

S WEET is true love though given in vain, in vain ;
And sweet is death who puts an end to pain :
I know not which is sweeter, no, not I.

Love, art thou sweet? then bitter death must be :
Love, thou art bitter ; sweet is death to me.
O Love, if death be sweeter, let me die.

Sweet love, that seems not made to fade away,
Sweet death that seems to make us loveless clay,
I know not which is sweeter, no, not I.

I fain would follow love, if that could be ;
I needs must follow death, who calls for me ;
Call and I follow, I follow ! let me die.

2

SONG OF THE NOVICE TO QUEEN GUINEVERE.

LATE, late, so late! and dark the night and chill!
Late, late, so late! but we can enter still.
Too late, too late! ye cannot enter now.

No light had we: for that we do repent;
And learning this, the bridegroom will relent.
Too late, too late! ye cannot enter now.

No light: so late! and dark and chill the night;
O let us in, that we may find the light!
Too late, too late: ye cannot enter now.

Have we not heard the bridegroom is so sweet?
O let us in, though late, to kiss his feet!
No, no, too late! ye cannot enter now.

RING OUT, WILD BELLS.

RING out, wild bells, to the wild sky,
The flying cloud, the frosty light;
The year is dying in the night;
Ring out, wild bells, and let him die.

Ring out the old, ring in the new,
    Ring, happy bells, across the snow:
    The year is going, let him go:
Ring out the false, ring in the true.

Ring out the grief that saps the mind,
    For those that here we see no more;
    Ring out the feud of rich and poor,
Ring in redress to all mankind.

Ring out a slowly dying cause,
    And ancient forms of party strife;
    Ring in the nobler modes of life,
With sweeter manners, purer laws.

Ring out the want, the care, the sin,
    The faithless coldness of the times;
    Ring out, ring out my mournful rhymes,
But ring the fuller minstrel in.

Ring out false pride in place and blood,
    The civic slander and the spite;
    Ring in the love of truth and right,
Ring in the common love of good.

Ring out old shapes of foul disease,
    Ring out the narrowing lust of gold;
    Ring out the thousand wars of old,
Ring in the thousand years of peace.

Ring in the valiant man and free,
    The larger heart, the kindlier hand;
    Ring out the darkness of the land,
Ring in the Christ that is to be.

BREAK, BREAK, BREAK.

Break, break, break,
   On thy cold gray stones, O Sea!
And I would that my tongue could utter
   The thoughts that arise in me.

O well for the fisherman's boy,
   That he shouts with his sister at play!
O well for the sailor lad,
   That he sings in his boat on the bay!

And the stately ships go on
  To their haven under the hill ;
But O for the touch of a vanished hand,
  And the sound of a voice that is still !

Break, break, break,
  At the foot of thy crags, O Sea !
But the tender grace of a day that is dead
  Will never come back to me.

COME NOT, WHEN I AM DEAD.

COME not, when I am dead,
    To drop thy foolish tears upon my grave,
To trample round my fallen head,
  And vex the unhappy dust thou would'st not save.
There let the wind sweep and the plover cry ;
      But thou, go by.

Child, if it were thine error or thy crime,
  I care no longer, being all unblest ;
Wed whom thou wilt, but I am sick of Time,
  And I desire to rest.
Pass on, weak heart, and leave me where I lie :
      Go by, go by.

THE POET'S SONG.

THE rain had fallen, the Poet arose,
  He passed by the town, and out of the street,
A light wind blew from the gates of the sun,
  And waves of shadow went over the wheat,
And he sat him down in a lonely place,
  And chanted a melody loud and sweet,
That made the wild-swan pause in her cloud,
  And the lark drop down at his feet.

The swallow stopt as he hunted the bee,
  The snake slipt under a spray,
The wild hawk stood with the down on his beak
  And stared, with his foot on the prey,
And the nightingale thought, "I have sung many songs,
  But never a one so gay,
For he sings of what the world will be
  When the years have died away."

LILIAN.

AIRY, fairy Lilian,
  Flitting, fairy Lilian,
When I ask her if she love me,
Clasps her tiny hands above me,
  Laughing all she can ;

She 'll not **tell me if she love me,**
    Cruel little Lilian.

    When my passion seeks
    Pleasance in love-sighs,
She, looking through and through me
Thoroughly to undo me,
    Smiling, never speaks :
So innocent-arch, so cunning-simple,
From beneath her gathered wimple
    Glancing with black-beaded eyes,
Till the lightning laughters dimple
        The baby-roses in **her** cheeks ;
        Then away she flies.

    Prithee weep, May Lilian !
        Gayety without eclipse
    Wearieth me, **May Lilian :**
Through my very heart it thrilleth
    When from crimson-threaded lips
Silver-treble laughter trilleth :
    Prithee weep, May Lilian.

        Praying all I can,
If prayers will not hush thee,
        Airy Lilian,
Like a rose-leaf I will **crush thee,**
        Fairy Lilian.

THE OWL.

WHEN cats run home and light is come,
    And dew is cold upon the ground,
And the far-off stream is dumb,
  And the whirring sail goes round,
  And the whirring sail goes round ;
    Alone and warming his five wits
    The white owl in the belfry sits.

When merry milkmaids click the latch,
  And rarely smells the new-mown hay,
And the cock hath sung beneath the thatch
  Twice or thrice his roundelay,
  Twice or thrice his roundelay ;
    Alone and warming his five wits
    The white owl in the belfry sits.

TO THE SAME.

THY tuwhits are lulled, I wot,
  Thy tuwhoos of yesternight,
Which upon the dark afloat,
  So took echo with delight,
  So took echo with delight,
    That her voice, untuneful grown,
    Wears all day a fainter tone.

I would mock thy chant anew ;
  But I cannot mimic it ;
Not a whit of thy tuwhoo,
  Thee to woo to thy tuwhit,
  Thee to woo to thy tuwhit,
    With a lengthened loud halloo,
    Tuwhoo, tuwhit, tuwhit, tuwhoo-o-o.

A SPIRIT HAUNTS.

I.

A SPIRIT haunts the year's last hours,
  Dwelling amid these yellowing bowers:
    To himself he talks;
For at eventide, listening earnestly,
At his work you may hear him sob and sigh
    In the walks;
    Earthward he boweth the heavy stalks
Of the mouldering flowers:
    Heavily **hangs** the broad sunflower
      Over its grave i' the earth so chilly;
    Heavily hangs the hollyhock,
      Heavily hangs the tiger-lily.

II.

The air is damp, and hushed, and close,
As a sick man's room when he taketh repose
    An hour before death;
My very heart faints and my whole soul grieves
At the moist rich smell of the rotting leaves,   .
    And the breath
    Of the fading edges of box beneath,
And the year's last rose.
    Heavily hangs the broad sunflower
      Over its grave i' the earth so chilly;
  .   Heavily hangs the hollyhock,
      Heavily hangs the tiger-lily.

CLARIBEL.

A MELODY.

WHERE Claribel low-lieth
    The breezes pause and die,
Letting the rose-leaves fall :
But the solemn oak-tree sigheth,
    Thick-leaved, ambrosial,

With an ancient melody
Of an inward agony,
Where Claribel low-lieth.

At eve the beetle boometh
  Athwart the thicket lone :
At noon the wild bee hummeth
  About the mossed headstone :
At midnight the moon cometh
  And looketh down alone.
Her song the lintwhite swelleth,
The clear-voiced mavis dwelleth,
  The callow throstle lispeth,
The slumbrous wave outwelleth,
  The babbling runnel crispeth,
The hollow grot replieth
Where Claribel low-lieth.

A DIRGE.

I.

NOW is done thy long day's work ;
  Fold thy palms across thy breast,
Fold thine arms, turn to thy rest.
    Let them rave.
Shadows of the silver birk
Sweep the green that folds thy grave.
    Let them rave.

II.

Thee nor carketh care nor slander ;
Nothing but the small cold worm

Fretteth thine enshrouded form.
  Let them rave.
Light and shadow ever wander
O'er the green that folds thy grave.
  Let them rave.

III.

Thou wilt not turn upon thy bed;
Chanteth not the brooding bee
Sweeter tones than calumny?
  Let them rave.
Thou wilt never raise thine head
From the green that folds thy grave.
  Let them rave.

IV.

Crocodiles wept tears for thee;
The woodbine and eglatere
Drip sweeter dews than traitor's tear.
  Let them rave.
Rain makes music in the tree
O'er the green that folds thy grave.
  Let them rave.

V.

Round thee blow, self-pleached deep
Bramble-roses, faint and pale,
And long purples of the dale.
  Let them rave.
These in every shower creep
Through the green that folds thy grave.
  Let them rave.

VI.

The gold-eyed kingcups fine,
The frail bluebell peereth over
Rare broidry of the purple clover.
    Let them rave.
Kings have no such couch as thine,
As the green that folds thy grave.
    Let them rave.

VII.

Wild words wander here and there;
God's great gift of speech abused
Makes thy memory confused, —
    But let them rave.
The balm-cricket carols clear
In the green that folds thy grave.
    Let them rave.

THE BALLAD OF ORIANA.

MY heart is wasted with my woe,
    Oriana.
There is no rest for me below,
    Oriana.
When the long dun wolds are ribbed with snow,
And loud the Norland whirlwinds blow,
    Oriana,
Alone I wander to and fro,
    Oriana.

Ere the light on dark was growing,
     Oriana,
At midnight the cock was crowing,
     Oriana:
Winds were blowing, waters flowing,
We heard the steeds to battle going,
     Oriana;
Aloud the hollow bugle blowing,
     Oriana.

In the yew-wood, black as night,
     Oriana,
Ere I rode into the fight,
     Oriana,
While blissful tears blinded my sight,
By star-shine and by moonlight,
     Oriana,
I to thee my troth did plight,
     Oriana.

She stood upon the castle wall,
     Oriana:
She watched my crest among them all,
     Oriana:
She saw me fight, she heard me call,
When forth there stept a foeman tall,
     Oriana,
Atween me and the castle wall,
     Oriana.

The bitter arrow went aside,
     Oriana:
The false, false arrow went aside,
     Oriana:

The damned arrow glanced aside,
And pierced thy heart, my love, my bride,
    Oriana!
Thy heart, my life, my love, my bride,
    Oriana!

O! narrow, narrow was the space,
    Oriana.
Loud, loud rung out the bugle's brays,
    Oriana.
O! deathful stabs were dealt apace,
The battle deepened in its place,
    Oriana;
But I was down upon my face,
    Oriana.

They should have stabbed me where I lay,
    Oriana!
How could I rise and come away,
    Oriana?
How could I look upon the day?
They should have stabbed me where I lay,
    Oriana, —
They should have trod me into clay,
    Oriana.

O! breaking heart that will not break,
    Oriana;
O! pale, pale face so sweet and meek,
    Oriana.
Thou smilest, but thou dost not speak,
And then the tears run down my cheek,
    Oriana:
What wantest thou? whom dost thou seek,
    Oriana?

I cry aloud : none hear my cries,
  Oriana.
Thou comest atween me and the skies,
  Oriana.
I feel the tears of blood arise
Up from my heart unto my eyes,
  Oriana.
Within thy heart my arrow lies,
  Oriana.

O cursed hand ! O cursed blow !
  Oriana !
O happy thou that liest low,
  Oriana !
All night the silence seems to flow
Beside me in my utter woe,
  Oriana.
A weary, weary way I go,
  Oriana.

When Norland winds pipe down the sea,
  Oriana,
I walk, I dare not think of thee,
  Oriana.
Thou liest beneath the greenwood tree,
I dare not die and come to thee,
  Oriana.
I hear the roaring of the sea,
  Oriana.

3

THE MILLER'S DAUGHTER.

IT is the miller's daughter,
  And she is grown so dear, so dear,
That I would be the jewel
  That trembles at her ear:

For, hid in ringlets day and night,
I 'd touch her neck so warm and white.

And I would be the girdle
  About her dainty, dainty waist,
And her heart would **beat against me**
  In sorrow and in rest :
And I should know if it beat right,
I 'd clasp it round **so close** and tight.

And I would be the necklace,
  And all day long to fall and rise
Upon her balmy bosom,
  With her laughter or her sighs,
And I would lie so light, so light,
  I scarce should be unclasped at night.

THE MERMAN.

WHO would be
  A merman bold
Sitting alone,
Singing **alone**
Under the sea,
With a crown of gold,
  On a throne ?

  I would be a merman bold ;
I would sit and sing the whole of the day ;
I would fill the sea-halls with a voice of power,
But at night I would roam abroad, and play

With the mermaids in and out of the rocks,
Dressing their hair with the white sea-flower;
And holding them back by their flowing locks,
I would kiss them often under the sea,
And kiss them again till they kissed me
    Laughingly, laughingly;
And then we would wander away, away
To the pale-green sea-groves straight and high,
    Chasing each other merrily.
There would be neither moon nor star;
But the wave would make music above us afar, —
Low thunder and light in the magic night, —
    Neither moon nor star.
We would call aloud in the dreamy dells,
Call to each other and whoop and cry
    All night, merrily, merrily;
They would pelt me with starry spangles and shells,
Laughing and clapping their hands between,
    All night, merrily, merrily;
But I would throw them back in mine
Turkis and agate and almondine:
Then leaping out upon them unseen,
I would kiss them often under the sea,
And kiss them again till they kissed me
    Laughingly, laughingly.
O! what a happy life were mine
Under the hollow-hung ocean green!
Soft are the moss-beds under the sea;
We would live merrily, merrily.

THE MERMAID.

WHO would be
A mermaid fair,
　Singing alone,
Combing her hair
Under the sea,
In a golden curl
With a comb of pearl,
　On a throne?

　I would be a mermaid fair;
I would sing to myself the whole of the day;
With a comb of pearl I would comb my hair;
And still as I combed I would sing and say,
" Who is it loves me? who loves not me?"
I would comb my hair till my ringlets would fall,
　　Low adown, low adown,
From under my starry sea-bud crown
　　Low adown and around,
And I should look like a fountain of gold
　　Springing alone
　　With a shrill inner sound
　　Over the throne
　　In the midst of the hall;
Till that great sea-snake under the sea
From his coiled sleeps in the central deeps
Would slowly trail himself sevenfold
Round the hall where I sate, and look in at the gate
With his large calm eyes for the love of me.

And all the mermen under the sea
Would feel their immortality
Die in their hearts for the love of me.

But at night I would wander away, away,
    I would fling on each side my low-flowing locks,
And lightly vault from the throne and play
    With the mermen in and out of the rocks;
We would run to and fro, and hide and seek,
    On the broad sea-wolds i' the crimson shells,
    Whose silvery spikes are nighest the sea.
But if any came near, I would call and shriek,
And adown the steep like a wave I would leap
    From the diamond ledges that jut from the dells,
For I would not be kissed by all who would list,
Of the bold merry mermen under the sea;
They would sue me, and woo me, and flatter me,
In the purple twilights under the sea;
But the king of them all would carry me,
Woo me, and win me, and marry me,
In the branching jaspers under the sea;
Then all the dry pied things that be
In the hueless mosses under the sea
Would curl round my silver feet silently,
All looking up for the love of me.
And if I should carol aloud, from aloft
All things that are forked, and horned, and soft,
Would lean out from the hollow sphere of the sea,
All looking down for the love of me.

THE SISTERS.

W E were two daughters of one race:
    She was the fairest in the face:
  The wind is blowing in turret and tree.
They were together, and she fell;
Therefore revenge became me well.
    O the Earl was fair to see!

She died: she went to burning flame:
She mixed her ancient blood with shame.
    The wind is howling in turret and tree.
Whole weeks and months, and early and late,
To win his love I lay in wait.
    O the Earl was fair to see!

I made a feast; I bade him come:
I won his love, I brought him home.
    The wind is roaring in turret and tree.
And after supper, on a bed,
Upon my lap he laid his head:
    O the Earl was so fair to see!

I kissed his eyelids into rest:
His ruddy cheek upon my breast.
    The wind is raging in turret and tree.
I hated him with the hate of hell,
But I loved his beauty passing well.
    O the Earl was fair to see!

I rose up in the silent night :
I made my dagger sharp and bright.
   The wind is raving in turret and tree.
As half-asleep his breath he drew,
Three times I stabbed him through and through.
   O the Earl was fair to see!

I curled and combed his comely head,
He looked so grand when he was dead.
   The wind is blowing in turret and tree.
I wrapt his body in the sheet,
And laid him at his mother's feet.
   O the Earl was fair to see!

LOVE THAT HATH US IN THE NET.

L OVE that hath us in the net,
   Can he pass, and we forget?
Many suns arise and set.
Many a chance the years beget.
Love the gift is Love the debt.
     Even so.
Love is hurt with jar and fret.
Love is made a vague regret.
Eyes with idle tears are wet.
Idle habit links us yet.
What is love? for we forget:
     Ah, no! no!

AS THRO' THE LAND AT EVE WE WENT.

A S thro' the land at eve we went,
  And pluck'd the ripen'd ears,
We fell out, my wife and I,
We fell out, I know not why,
  And kiss'd again with tears.

And blessings on the falling out
  That all the more endears,
When we fall out with those we love,
  And kiss again with tears !

For when we came where lies the child
  We lost in other years,
There above the little grave,
O there above the little grave,
  We kiss'd again with tears.

SWEET AND LOW.

SWEET and low, sweet and low,
  Wind of the western sea,
Low, low, breathe and blow,
  Wind of the western sea !
Over the rolling waters go,
Come from the dying moon, and blow,
  Blow him again to me ;
While my little one, while my pretty one, sleeps.

Sleep and rest, sleep and rest,
  Father will come to thee soon ;
Rest, rest, on mother's breast,
  Father will come to thee soon ;
Father will come to his babe in the nest,
Silver sails all out of the west,
  Under the silver moon ;
Sleep, my little one, sleep, my pretty one, sleep.

THY VOICE IS HEARD.

THY voice is heard through rolling drums
　　That beat to battle where he stands ;
Thy face across his fancy comes,
　And gives the battle to his hands :
A moment, while the trumpets blow,
　He sees his brood about thy knee ;
The next, like fire he meets the foe,
　And strikes him dead for thine and thee.

LADY CLARA VERE DE VERE.

LADY Clara Vere de Vere,
　　Of me you shall not win renown ;
You thought to break a country heart
　For pastime, ere you went to town.
At me you smiled, but unbeguiled
　I saw the snare, and I retired :
The daughter of a hundred Earls,
　You are not one to be desired.

Lady Clara Vere de Vere,
　I know you proud to bear your name ;
Your pride is yet no mate for mine,
　Too proud to care from whence I came.

Nor would I break for your sweet sake
   A heart that dotes on truer charms.
A simple maiden in her flower
   Is worth a hundred coats-of-arms.

Lady Clara Vere de Vere,
   Some meeker pupil you must find,
For were you queen of all that is,
   I could not stoop to such a mind.
You sought to prove how I could love,
   And my disdain is my reply.
The lion on your old stone gates .
   Is not more cold to you than I.

Lady Clara Vere de Vere,
   You put strange memories in my head.
Not thrice your branching limes have blown
   Since I beheld young Laurence dead.
O your sweet eyes, your low replies:
   A great enchantress you may be;
But there was that across his throat
   Which you had hardly cared to see.

Lady Clara Vere de Vere,
   When thus he met his mother's view,
She had the passions of her kind,
   She spake some certain truths of you.
Indeed, I heard one bitter word
   That scarce is fit for you to hear:
Her manners had not that repose
   Which stamps the caste of Vere de Vere.

Lady Clara Vere de Vere,
   There stands a spectre in your hall:

The guilt of blood is at your door:
    You changed a wholesome heart to gall,
You held your course without remorse,
    To make him trust his modest worth,
And, last, you fixed a vacant stare,
    And slew him with your noble birth.

Trust me, Clara Vere de Vere,
    From yon blue heavens above us bent
The grand old gardener and his wife
    Smile at the claims of long descent.
Howe'er it be, it seems to me,
    'T is only noble to be good.
Kind hearts are more than coronets,
    And simple faith than Norman blood.

I know you, Clara Vere de Vere:
    You pine among your halls and towers;
The languid light of your proud eyes
    Is wearied of the rolling hours.
In glowing health, with boundless wealth,
    But sickening of a vague disease,
You know so ill to deal with time,
    You needs must play such pranks as these.

Clara, Clara Vere de Vere,
    If Time be heavy on your hands,
Are there no beggars at your gate,
    Nor any poor about your lands?
O! teach the orphan-boy to read,
    Or teach the orphan-girl to sew,
Pray Heaven for a human heart,
    And let the foolish yeoman go.

THE DEATH OF THE OLD YEAR.

FULL knee-deep lies the winter snow,
  And the winter winds are wearily sighing:
Toll ye the church-bell sad and slow,
And tread softly and speak low,
For the old year lies a-dying.
    Old year, you must not die;
    You came to us so readily,
    You lived with us so steadily,
    Old year, you shall not die.

He lieth still: he doth not move:
He will not see the dawn of day.
He hath no other life above.
He gave me a friend, and a true, true-love,
And the New-year will take 'em away.
    Old year, you must not go;
    So long as you have been with us,
    Such joy as you have seen with us,
    Old year, you shall not go.

He frothed his bumpers to the brim;
A jollier year we shall not see.
But though his eyes are waxing dim,
And though his foes speak ill of him,
He was a friend to me.
    Old year, you shall not die;
    We did so laugh and cry with you,
    I 've half a mind to die with you,
    Old year, if you must die.

He was full of joke and jest,
But all his merry quips are o'er.
To see him die, across the waste
His son and heir doth ride post-haste,
But he 'll be dead before.
  Every one for his **own.**
  The night is starry and cold, my friend,
  And the New-year, blithe and bold, my friend
  Comes up to take his own.

How hard he breathes! over the snow
I heard just now **the crowing cock.**
The shadows flicker to and fro:
The cricket chirps: the light burns low:
'T is nearly twelve o'clock.
  Shake hands before you die.
  Old year, we 'll dearly rue for **you:**
  What is it we can do for you?
  Speak out before you die.

His face is growing **sharp and** thin.
Alack! our friend is gone.
Close up his eyes: tie up his chin:
Step from the corpse, and let him in
That standeth there alone,
  And waiteth at the door.
  There 's a new foot on the floor, my friend,
  And a new face at the door, my friend,
  A new face at the door.

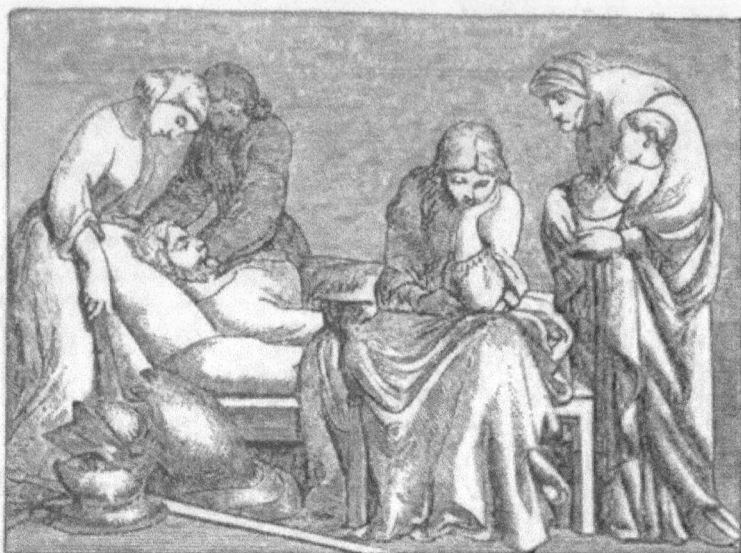

HOME THEY BROUGHT HER WARRIOR DEAD.

H OME they brought her warrior dead:
 She nor swooned nor uttered cry:
All her maidens, watching, said,
 " She must weep or she will die."

Then they praised him, soft and low,
 Called him worthy to be loved,
Truest friend and noblest foe;
 Yet she neither spoke nor moved.

Stole a maiden from her place,
 Lightly to the warrior stept,
Took the face-cloth from the face:
 Yet she neither moved nor wept.

Rose a nurse of ninety years,
　　Set his child upon her knee, —
Like summer tempest came her tears, —
　　" Sweet my child, I live for thee."

OUR ENEMIES HAVE FALLEN.

OUR enemies have fallen, have fallen : the **seed**,
　　The little seed they laughed at in the dark,
Has risen and cleft the soil, and grown a bulk
Of spanless girth, that lays on every side
A thousand arms and rushes to the Sun.

　Our enemies have fallen, have **fallen** : they came ;
The leaves were wet with women's **tears** ; they **heard**
A noise of songs they **would not** understand.
They marked it with the red **cross to the fall**,
And would have **strown it, and are fallen themselves.**

　Our enemies have fallen, have fallen : **they came,**
The woodmen with their axes : lo the tree !
But we will make it fagots for the hearth,
And shape it plank and beam for roof and floor,
And boats and bridges for the use of men.

　Our enemies have fallen, have fallen : they **struck** ;
With their own blows they hurt themselves, nor **knew**
There dwelt an iron nature in the grain :
The glittering axe was **broken in** their arms,
Their arms were shattered to the shoulder-blade.

4

Our enemies have fallen, but this shall grow
A night of Summer from the heat, a breadth
Of Autumn, dropping fruits of power ; and rolled
With music in the growing breeze of Time,
The tops shall strike from star to star, the fangs
Shall move the stony bases of the world.

THE MAY QUEEN.

I.

YOU must wake and call me early, call me early, mother dear ;
    To-morrow 'ill be the happiest time of all the glad New-
      year ;
Of all the glad New-year, mother, the maddest, merriest day ;
For I 'm to be Queen o' the May, mother, I 'm to be Queen o'
    the May.

II.

There 's many a black, black eye, they say, but none so bright as
    mine ;
There 's Margaret and Mary, there 's Kate and Caroline :
But none so fair as little Alice in all the land, they say :
So I 'm to be Queen o' the May, mother, I 'm to be Queen o'
    the May.

III.

I sleep so sound all night, mother, that I shall never wake,
If you do not call me loud when the day begins to break :
But I must gather knots of flowers, and buds and garlands gay,
For I 'm to be Queen of the May, mother, I 'm to be Queen o'
    the May.

IV.

As I came up the valley, whom think ye should I see,
But Robin leaning on the bridge beneath the hazel-tree?
He thought of that sharp look, mother, I gave him yesterday, —
But I 'm to be Queen o' the May, mother, I 'm to be Queen o'
    the May.

V.

He thought I was a ghost, mother, for I was all in white,
And I ran by him without speaking, like a flash of light.
They call me cruel-hearted, but I care not what they say,
For I 'm to be Queen o' the May, mother, I 'm to be Queen o'
    the May.

VI.

They say he 's dying all for love, but that can never be :
They say his heart is breaking, mother, — what is that to me?
There 's many a bolder lad 'ill woo me any summer day,
And I 'm to be Queen o' the May, mother, I 'm to be Queen o'
    the May.

VII.

Little Effie shall go with me to-morrow to the green,
And you 'll be there, too, mother, to see me made the Queen :
For the shepherd lads on every side 'ill come from far away,
And I 'm to be Queen o' the May, mother, I 'm to be Queen o'
    the May.

VIII.

The honeysuckle round the porch has woven its wavy bowers,
And by the meadow-trenches blow the faint sweet cuckoo-flowers ;
And the wild marsh-marigold shines like fire in swamps and
    hollows gray,
And I 'm to be Queen o' the May, mother, I 'm to be Queen o'
    the May.

IX.

The night-winds come and go, mother, upon the meadow grass,
And the happy stars above them seem to brighten as they pass;
There will not be a drop of rain the whole of the livelong day,
And I'm to be Queen o' the May, mother, I'm to be Queen o'
 the May.

X.

All the valley, mother, 'ill be fresh and green and still,
And the cowslip and the crowfoot are over all the hill,
And the rivulet in the flowery dale 'ill merrily glance and play,
For I'm to be Queen o' the May, mother, I'm to be Queen o'
 the May.

XI.

So you must wake and call me early, call me early, mother dear,
To-morrow 'ill be the happiest time of all the glad New-year:
To-morrow 'ill be of all the year the maddest, merriest day,
For I'm to be Queen o' the May, mother, I'm to be Queen o'
 the May.

NEW YEAR'S EVE.

I.

IF you're waking call me early, call me early, mother dear,
 For I would see the sun rise upon the glad New-year.
It is the last New-year that I shall ever see,
Then you may lay me low i' the mould, and think no more of me.

II.

To-night I saw the sun set: he set and left behind
The good old year, the dear old time, and all my peace of mind;
And the New-year's coming up, mother, but I shall never see
The blossom on the blackthorn, the leaf upon the tree.

III.

Last May we made a crown of flowers : we had a merry day ;
Beneath the hawthorn on the green they made me Queen of May ;
And we danced about the May-pole and in the hazel copse,
Till Charles's Wain came out above the tall white chimney-tops.

IV.

There 's not a flower on all the hills : the frost is on the pane :
I only wish to live till the snowdrops come again :
I wish the snow would melt and the sun come out on high :
I long to see a flower so before the day I die.

V.

The building rook 'ill caw from the windy tall elm-tree,
And the tufted plover pipe along the fallow lea,
And the swallow 'ill come back again with summer o'er the wave,
But I shall lie alone, mother, within the mouldering grave.

VI.

Upon the chancel-casement, and upon that grave of mine,
In the early, early morning the summer sun 'ill shine,
Before the red cock crows from the farm upon the hill,
When you are warm asleep, mother, and all the world is still.

VII.

When the flowers come again, mother, beneath the waning light,
You 'll never see me more in the long gray fields at night;
When from the dry dark wold the summer airs blow cool
On the oat-grass and the sword-grass, and the bulrush in the
      pool.

VIII.

You 'll bury me, my mother, just beneath the hawthorn shade,
And you 'll come sometimes and see me where I am lowly laid.

I shall not forget you, mother, I shall hear you when you pass,
With your feet above my head in the long and pleasant grass.

IX.

I have been wild and wayward, but you 'll forgive me now;
You 'll kiss me, my own mother, and forgive me ere I go:
Nay, nay, you must not weep, nor let your grief be wild,
You should not fret for me, mother, you have another child.

X.

If I can, I 'll come again, mother, from out my resting-place;
Though you 'll not see me, mother, I shall look upon your face;
Though I cannot speak a word, I shall hearken what you say,
And be often, often with you when you think I 'm far away.

XI.

Good night, good night, when I have said good night forever-
        more,
And you see me carried out from the threshold of the door;
Don't let Effie come to see me till my grave be growing green:
She 'll be a better child to you than ever I have been.

XII.

She 'll find my garden-tools upon the granary floor;
Let her take 'em: they are hers: I shall never garden more:
But tell her, when I 'm gone, to train the rose-bush that I set
About the parlor-window and the box of mignonette.

XIII.

Good night, sweet mother: call me before the day is born.
All night I lie awake, but I fall asleep at morn;
But I would see the sun rise upon the glad New-year,
So, if you 're waking, call me, call me early, mother dear.

CONCLUSION.

I.

I THOUGHT to pass away before, and yet alive I am;
And in the fields all round I hear the bleating of the lamb.
How sadly, I remember, rose the morning of the year!
To die before the snowdrop came, and now the violet 's here.

II.

O sweet is the new violet, that comes beneath the skies,
And sweeter is the young lamb's voice to me that cannot rise,
And sweet is all the land about, and all the flowers that blow,
And sweeter far is death than life to me that long to go.

III.

It seemed so hard at first, mother, to leave the blessed sun,
And now it seems as hard to stay ; and yet, His will be done !
But still I think it can't be long before I find release ;
And that good man, the clergyman, has told me words of peace.

IV.

O blessings on his kindly voice and on his silver hair !
And blessings on his whole life long, until he meet me there !
O blessings on his kindly heart and on his silver head !
A thousand times I blest him, as he knelt beside my bed.

V.

He taught me all the mercy, for he showed me all the sin.
Now, though my lamp was lighted late, there's One will let me in :
Nor would I now be well, mother, again, if that could be,
For my desire is but to pass to Him that died for me.

VI.

I did not hear the dog howl, mother, or the death-watch beat,
There came a sweeter token when the night and morning meet :
But sit beside my bed, mother, and put your hand in mine,
And Effie on the other side, and I will tell the sign.

VII.

All in the wild March-morning I heard the angels call ;
It was when the moon was setting, and the dark was over all ;
The trees began to whisper, and the wind began to roll,
And in the wild March-morning I heard them call my soul.

VIII.

For lying broad awake I thought of you and Effie dear;
I saw you sitting in the house, and I no longer here;
With all my strength I prayed for both, and so I felt resigned,
And up the valley came a swell of music on the wind.

IX.

I thought that it was fancy, and I listened in my bed,
And then did something speak to me — I know not what was
       said;
For great delight and shuddering took hold of all my mind,
And up the valley came again the music on the wind.

X.

But you were sleeping; and I said, "It's not for them; it's
       mine."
And if it comes three times, I thought, I take it for a sign.
And once again it came, and close beside the window-bars,
Then seemed to go right up to heaven and die among the stars.

XI.

So now I think my time is near. I trust it is. I know
The blessed music went that way my soul will have to go.
And for myself, indeed, I care not if I go to-day,
But, Effie, you must comfort *her* when I am passed away.

XII.

And say to Robin a kind word, and tell him not to fret;
There 's many worthier than I would make him happy yet.
If I had lived — I cannot tell — I might have been his wife;
But all these things have ceased to be, with my desire of life.

XIII.

O look! the sun begins to rise, the heavens are in a glow;
He shines upon a hundred fields, and all of them I know.

And there I move no longer now, and there his light may shine —
Wild flowers in the valley for other hands than mine.

XIV.

O sweet and strange it seems to me, that ere this day is done
The voice that now is speaking may be beyond the sun —
Forever and forever with those just souls and true —
And what is life, that we should moan ? why make we such ado ?

XV.

Forever and forever, all in a blessed home —
And there to wait a little while till you and Effie come —
To lie within the light of God, as I lie upon your breast —
And the wicked cease from troubling, and the weary are at rest.

THE SEA-FAIRIES.

SLOW sailed the weary mariners, and saw,
  Betwixt the green brink and the running foam,
Sweet faces, rounded arms, and bosoms prest
To little harps of gold ; and, while they mused,
Whispering to each other half in fear,
Shrill music reached them on the middle sea.

Whither away, whither away, whither away ? fly no more.
Whither away from the high green field, and the happy blossoming
      shore ?
Day and night to the billow the fountain calls ;
Down shower the gambolling waterfalls
From wandering over the lea :

Out of the live-green heart of the dells
They freshen the silvery-crimson shells,
And thick with white bells the clover-hill swells
High over the full-toned sea:
O hither, come hither, and furl your sails,
Come hither to me and to me!
Hither, come hither, and frolic and play;   ,
Here it is only the mew that wails;
We will sing to you all the day:
Mariner, mariner, furl your sails,
For here are the blissful downs and dales,
And merrily, merrily carol the gales,
And the spangle dances in bight and bay,
And the rainbow forms and flies on the land
Over the islands free;
And the rainbow lives in the curve of the sand;
Hither, come hither and see;
And the rainbow hangs on the poising wave,
And sweet is the color of cove and cave,
And sweet shall your welcome be;
O hither, come hither, and be our lords,
For merry brides are we!
We will kiss sweet kisses, and speak sweet words:
O listen, listen, your eyes shall glisten
With pleasure and love and jubilee!
O listen, listen, your eyes shall glisten
When the sharp, clear twang of the golden chords
Runs up the ridgéd sea!
Who can light on as happy a shore
All the world o'er, all the world o'er?
Whither away? listen and stay: mariner, mariner fly no more.

THE DESERTED HOUSE.

I.

LIFE and Thought have gone away
      Side by side,
Leaving door and windows wide:
Careless tenants they!

II.

All within is dark as night:
In the windows is no light;
And no murmur at the door,
So frequent on its hinge before.

III.

Close the door, the shutters close,
      Or through the windows we shall see
      The nakedness and vacancy
Of the dark, deserted house.

IV.

Come away; no more of mirth
      Is here or merry-making sound.
The house was builded of the earth,
      And shall fall again to ground.

V.

Come away; for Life and Thought
      Here no longer dwell;
      But in a city glorious —
A great and distant city — have bought
      A mansion incorruptible,
      Would they could have stayed with us.

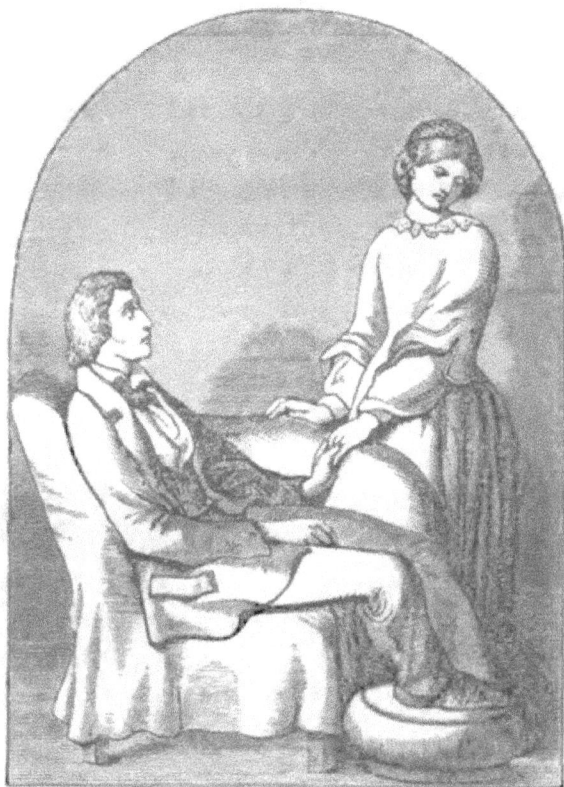

ASK ME NO MORE.

A SK me no more: the moon may draw the sea;
The cloud may stoop from heaven and take the shape,
With fold to fold, of mountain or of cape;
But, O too fond, when have I answered thee?
Ask me no more.

Ask me no more: what answer should I give?
I love not hollow cheek or faded eye:
Yet, O my friend, I will not have thee die!

Ask me no more, lest I should bid thee live;
    Ask me no more.

Ask me no more: thy fate and mine are sealed:
I strove against the stream and all in vain:
Let the great river take me to the main:
No more, dear love, for at a touch I yield;
    Ask me no more.

NOW SLEEPS THE CRIMSON PETAL.

NOW sleeps the crimson petal, now the white,
    Nor waves the cypress in the palace walk;
Nor winks the goldfin in the porphyry font:
The fire-fly wakens: waken thou with me.

Now droops the milk-white peacock like a ghost,
And like a ghost she glimmers on to me.

Now lies the Earth all Danaë to the stars,
And all thy heart lies open unto me.

Now slides the silent meteor on, and leaves
A shining furrow, as thy thoughts in me.

Now folds the lily all her sweetness up,
And slips into the bosom of the lake:
So fold thyself, my dearest, thou, and slip
Into my bosom and be lost in me.

COME DOWN, O MAID.

COME down, O maid, from yonder mountain height:
What pleasure lives in height, (the shepherd sang,)
In height and cold, the splendor of the hills?
But cease to move so near the heavens, and cease
To glide a sunbeam by the blasted pine,
To sit a star upon the sparkling spire;
And come, for Love is of the valley, come,
For Love is of the valley, come thou down
And find him; by the happy threshold, he,
Or hand in hand with Plenty in the maize,
Or red with spirted purple of the vats,
Or fox-like in the vine; nor cares to walk
With Death and Morning on the Silver Horns,
Nor wilt thou snare him in the white ravine,
Nor find him dropt upon the firths of ice,
That huddling slant in furrow-cloven falls
To roll the torrent out of dusky doors:
But follow; let the torrent dance thee down
To find him in the valley; let the wild
Lean-headed eagles yelp alone, and leave
The monstrous ledges there to slope, and spill
Their thousand wreaths of dangling water-smoke,
That like a broken purpose waste in air:
So waste not thou; but come; for all the vales
Await thee; azure pillars of the hearth
Arise to thee; the children call, and I
Thy shepherd pipe, and sweet is every sound,
Sweeter thy voice, but every sound is sweet;

Myriads of rivulets hurrying through the lawn,
The moan of doves in immemorial elms,
And murmuring of innumerable bees.

THE GOLDEN YEAR.

WE sleep and wake and sleep, but all things move;
    The Sun flies forward to his brother Sun;
The dark Earth follows wheeled in her ellipse:
And human things returning on themselves
Move onward, leading up the golden year.

Ah, though the times when some new thought can bud
Are but as poets' seasons when they flower,
Yet seas that daily gain upon the shore
Have ebb and flow conditioning their march,
And slow and sure comes up the golden year.

When wealth no more shall rest in mounded heaps,
But smit with freer light shall slowly melt
In many streams to fatten lower lands,
And light shall spread, and man be liker man
Through all the season of the golden year.

Shall eagles not be eagles? wrens be wrens?
If all the world were falcons, what of that?
The wonder of the eagle were the less,
But he not less the eagle.   Happy days
Roll onward, leading up the golden year.

Fly, happy, happy sails, and bear the Press;
Fly happy with the mission of the Cross;
Knit land to land, and blowing havenward.
With silks, and fruits, and spices, clear of toll,
Enrich the markets of the golden year.

But we grow old. Ah! when shall all men's good
Be each man's rule, and universal Peace
Lie like a shaft of light across the land,
And like a lane of beams athwart the sea,
Through all the circle of the golden year?

ST. AGNES' EVE.

I.

DEEP on the convent-roof the snows
  Are sparkling to the moon:
My breath to heaven like vapor goes:
  May my soul follow soon!
The shadows of the convent-towers
  Slant down the snowy sward,
Still creeping with the creeping hours
  That lead me to my Lord:
Make Thou my spirit pure and clear
  As are the frosty skies,
Or this first snowdrop of the year
  That in my bosom lies.

5

II.

As these white robes are soiled and dark,
  To yonder shining ground ;
As this pale taper's earthly spark,
  To yonder argent round ;
So shows my soul before the Lamb,
  My spirit before Thee ;
So in mine earthly house I am,
  To that I hope to be.
Break up the heavens, O Lord ! and far,
  Through all yon starlight keen,
Draw me, thy bride, a glittering star,
  In raiment white and clean.

III.

He lifts me to the golden doors ;
  The flashes come and go ;
All heaven bursts her starry floors,
  And strews her lights below,
And deepens on and up ! the gates
  Roll back, and far within
For me the Heavenly Bridegroom waits,
  To make me pure of sin.
The sabbaths of Eternity,
  One sabbath deep and wide —
A light upon the shining sea —
  The Bridegroom with his bride !

A FAREWELL.

FLOW down, cold rivulet, to the sea,
  Thy tribute wave deliver:
No more by thee my steps shall be,
  Forever and forever.

Flow, softly flow, by lawn and lea,
  A rivulet then a river:
Nowhere by thee my steps shall be,
  Forever and forever.

But here will sigh thine alder-tree,
  And here thine aspen shiver;
And here by thee will hum the bee
  Forever and forever.

A thousand suns will stream on thee,
  A thousand moons will quiver;
But not by thee my steps shall be,
  Forever and forever.

THE BEGGAR MAID.

HER arms across her breast she laid;
    She was more fair than words can say:
Barefooted came the beggar maid
    Before the King Cophetua.
In robe and crown the king stept down,
    To meet and greet her on her way;
"It is no wonder," said the lords,
    "She is more beautiful than day."

As shines the moon in clouded skies,
    She in her poor attire was seen:
One praised her ankles, one her eyes,
    One her dark hair and lovesome mien.
So sweet a face, such angel grace,
    In all that land had never been:
Cophetua sware a royal oath:
    "This beggar maid shall be my queen!"

MOVE EASTWARD, HAPPY EARTH.

MOVE eastward, happy earth, and leave
    Yon orange sunset waning slow;
From fringes of the faded eve,
  O, happy planet, eastward go;
Till over thy dark shoulder glow
  Thy silver sister-world, and rise

To glass herself in dewy eyes
That watch me from the glen below.

Ah, bear me with thee, smoothly borne,
Dip forward under starry light,
And move me to my marriage-morn,
And round again to happy night.

THE SKIPPING-ROPE.

SURE never yet was Antelope
  Could skip so lightly by.
Stand off, or else my skipping-rope
  Will hit you in the eye.

How lightly whirls the skipping-rope!
  How fairy-like you fly!
Go, get you gone, you muse and mope,—
  I hate that silly sigh.
Nay, dearest, teach me how to hope,
  Or tell me how to die.
There, take it, take my skipping-rope
  And hang yourself thereby.

THE SAILOR-BOY.

H E rose at dawn, and, fired with hope,
    Shot o'er the seething harbor-bar,
And reach'd the ship and caught the rope,
    And whistled to the morning star.

And while he whistled long and loud,
    He heard a fierce mermaiden cry,
" O boy, tho' thou art young and proud,
    I see the place where thou wilt lie.

" The sands and yeasty surges mix
    In caves about the dreary bay,
And on thy ribs the limpet sticks,
    And in thy heart the scrawl shall play."

" Fool," he answer'd, " death is sure
    To those that stay and those that roam,
But I will nevermore endure
    To sit with empty hands at home.

" My mother clings about my neck,
    My sisters crying ' stay for shame' ;
My father raves of death and wreck,
    They are all to blame, they are all to blame.

" God help me ! save I take my part
    Of danger on the roaring sea,
A devil rises in my heart,
    Far worse than any death to me."

THE ISLET.

"WHITHER, O whither, love, shall we go,
    For a score of sweet little summers or so,"
The sweet little wife of the singer said,
On the day that follow'd the day she was wed,
"Whither, O whither, love, shall we go ? "
And the singer shaking his curly head
Turn'd as he sat, and struck the keys
There at his right with a sudden crash,
Singing, "And shall it be over the seas
With a crew that is neither rude nor rash,
But a bevy of Eroses apple-cheek'd,
In a shallop of crystal ivory-beak'd,
With a satin sail of a ruby glow,
To a sweet little Eden on earth that I know,
A mountain islet pointed and peak'd ;
Waves on a diamond shingle dash,
Cataract brooks to the ocean run,
Fairily-delicate palaces shine
Mixt with myrtle and clad with vine,
And overstream'd and silvery-streak'd
With many a rivulet high against the Sun
The facets of the glorious mountain flash
Above the valleys of palm and pine."

"Thither, O thither, love, let us go."

"No, no, no !
For in all that exquisite isle, my dear,

There is but one bird with a musical throat,
And his compass is but of a single note,
That it makes one weary to hear."

"Mock me not! mock me not! love, let us go."

"No, love, no.
For the bud ever breaks into bloom on the tree,
And a storm never wakes on the lonely sea,
And a worm is there in the lonely wood,
That pierces the liver and blackens the blood,
And makes it a sorrow to be."

THE RINGLET.

"YOUR ringlets, your ringlets,
  That look so golden-gay,
If you will give me one, but one,
  To kiss it night and day,
Then never chilling touch of Time
  Will turn it silver-gray;
And then shall I know it is all true gold
To flame and sparkle and stream as of old,
Till all the comets in heaven are cold,
  And all her stars decay."
"Then take it, love, and put it by;
This cannot change, nor yet can I."

2.

"My ringlet, my ringlet,
  That art so golden-gay,
Now never chilling touch of Time
  Can turn thee silver-gray;
And a lad may wink, and a girl may hint,
  And a fool may say his say;
For my doubts and fears were all amiss,
And I swear henceforth by this and this,
That a doubt will only come for a kiss,
  And a fear to be kiss'd away."
"Then kiss it, love, and put it by:
If this can change, why so can I."

II.

O Ringlet, O Ringlet,
  I kiss'd you night and day,
And Ringlet, O Ringlet,
  You still are golden-gay,
But Ringlet, O Ringlet,
  You should be silver-gray:
For what is this which now I'm told,
I that took you for true gold,
She that gave you's bought and sold,
      Sold, sold.

2.

O Ringlet, O Ringlet,
  She blush'd a rosy red,
When Ringlet, O Ringlet,
  She clipt you from her head,
And Ringlet, O Ringlet,

She gave you me, and said,
"Come, kiss it, love, and put it by;
If this can change, why so can I."
O fie, you golden nothing, fie
     You golden lie.

3.

O Ringlet, O Ringlet,
   I count you much **to blame,**
For Ringlet, O Ringlet,
   You put me much to **shame,**
So Ringlet, O Ringlet,
   I doom you to the flame.
For what is this which **now I learn,**
Has given all my faith a turn ?
Burn, you glossy heretic, **burn,**
    Burn, burn.

THE BROOK.

I COME from haunts of coot and hern,
   I make a sudden sally
And sparkle out among the **fern,**
   To bicker down a valley.

By thirty hills I hurry down,
   Or slip between the ridges,
By twenty thorps, a little town,
   And **half a** hundred bridges.

Till last by Philip's farm I flow
To join the brimming river,
For men may come and men may go,
But I go on forever.

I chatter over stony ways,
   In little sharps and trebles,
I bubble into eddying bays,
   I babble on the pebbles.

With many a curve my banks I fret
   By many a field and fallow,
And many a fairy foreland set
   With willow-weed and mallow.

I chatter, chatter, as I flow
   To join the brimming river,
For men may come and men may go,
   But I go on forever.

I wind about, and in and out,
   With here a blossom sailing,
And here and there a lusty trout,
   And here and there a grayling,

And here and there a foamy flake
   Upon me, as I travel,
With many a silvery waterbreak
   Above the golden gravel,

And draw them all along, and flow
   To join the brimming river,
For men may come and men may go,
   But I go on forever.

I steal by lawns and grassy plots,
   I slide by hazel covers;
I move the sweet forget-me-nots
   That grow for happy lovers.

I slip, I slide, I gloom, I glance,
   Among my skimming swallows;
I make the netted sunbeam dance
   Against my sandy shallows.

I murmur under moon and stars
   In brambly wildernesses;
I linger by my shingly bars;
   I loiter round my cresses;

And out again I curve and flow
   To join the brimming river,
For men may come and men may go,
   But I go on forever.

A WELCOME TO ALEXANDRA.

MARCH 7, 1863.

SEA-KINGS' daughter from over the sea,
             Alexandra!
Saxon and Norman and Dane are we,
But all of us Danes in our welcome of thee,
             Alexandra!
Welcome her, thunders of fort and of fleet!
Welcome her, thundering cheer of the street!
Welcome her, all things youthful and sweet,
Scatter the blossom under her feet!

Break, happy land, into earlier flowers!
Make music, O bird, in the new-budded bowers!
Blazon your mottos of blessing and prayer!
Welcome her, welcome her, all that is ours!
Warble, O bugle, and trumpet, blare!
Flags, flutter out upon turrets and towers!
Flames, on the windy headland flare!
Utter your jubilee, steeple and spire!
Clash, ye bells, in the merry March air!
Flash, ye cities, in rivers of fire!
Rush to the roof, sudden rocket, and higher
Melt into stars for the land's desire!
Roll and rejoice, jubilant voice,
Roll as a ground-swell dash'd on the strand,
Roar as the sea when he welcomes the land,
And welcome her, welcome the land's desire,
The sea-kings' daughter as happy as fair,
Blissful bride of a blissful heir,
Bride of the heir of the kings of the sea, —
O joy to the people and joy to the throne,
Come to us, love us, and make us your own:
For Saxon or Dane or Norman we,
Teuton or Celt, or whatever we be,
We are each all Dane in our welcome of thee,

Alexandra!

ODE

SUNG AT THE OPENING OF THE INTERNATIONAL EXHIBITION.

UPLIFT a thousand voices full and sweet,
   In this wide hall with earth's inventions stored,
  And praise th' invisible universal Lord,
Who lets once more in peace the nations meet,
   Where Science, Art, and Labor have outpour'd
Their myriad horns of plenty at our feet.

O silent father of our Kings to be
Mourn'd in this golden hour of jubilee,
For this, for all, we weep our thanks to thee!

      The world-compelling plan was thine,
      And, lo! the long laborious miles
      Of Palace; lo! the giant aisles,
      Rich in model and design;
      Harvest-tool and husbandry,
      Loom and wheel and engin'ry,
      Secrets of the sullen mine,
      Steel and gold, and corn and wine,
      Fabric rough, or Fairy fine,
      Sunny tokens of the Line,
      Polar marvels, and a feast
      Of wonder, out of West and East,
      And shapes and hues of Part divine!
      All of beauty, all of use,
      That one fair planet can produce.

Brought from under every star,
Blown from over every main,
And mixt, as life is mixt with pain,
The works of peace with works of war.

O ye, the wise who think, the wise who reign,
From growing commerce loose her latest chain,
And let the fair white-wing'd peacemaker fly
To happy havens under all the sky,
And mix the seasons and the golden hours,
Till each man finds his own in all men's good,
And all men work in noble brotherhood,
Breaking their mailed fleets and armed towers,
And ruling by obeying Nature's powers,
And gathering all the fruits of peace and crown'd with all her
     flowers.

MY LIFE IS FULL OF WEARY DAYS.

MY life is full of weary days,
  But good things have not kept aloof,
Nor wandered into other ways:
  I have not lack'd thy mild reproof,
Nor golden largess of thy praise.

And now shake hands across the brink
  Of that deep grave to which I go:
Shake hands once more: I cannot sink
  So far — far down, but I shall know
  Thy voice, and answer from below.

HOME THEY BROUGHT HIM SLAIN WITH SPEARS.

HOME they brought him slain with spears,
  They brought him home at even-fall:
All alone she sits and hears
  Echoes in his empty hall,
    Sounding on the morrow.

The Sun peep'd in from open field,
  The boy began to leap and prance,
  Rode upon his father's lance,
Beat upon his father's shield, —
    "O hush, my joy, my sorrow."

CRADLE SONG.

W HAT does little birdie say
    In her nest at peep of day?
Let me fly, says little birdie,
Mother, let me fly away.

Birdie, rest a little longer,
Till the little wings are stronger.
So she rests a little longer,
Then she flies away.

What does little baby say,
In her bed at peep of day?
Baby says, like little birdie,
Let me rise and fly away.
Baby sleep a little longer,
Till the little limbs are stronger.
If she sleeps a little longer
Baby too shall fly away.

Cambridge : Electrotyped and Printed by Welch, Bigelow, & Co.

BY

ROBERT BROWNING.

WITH ILLUSTRATIONS BY S. EYTINGE, JR.

BOSTON:
JAMES R. OSGOOD AND COMPANY,
LATE TICKNOR & FIELDS, AND FIELDS, OSGOOD, & CO.
1871.

UNIVERSITY PRESS: WELCH, BIGELOW, & CO.,
CAMBRIDGE.

CONTENTS.

LYRICS OF LIFE.

—◆—

"HEAP CASSIA, SANDAL-BUDS, AND STRIPES."

HEAP cassia, sandal-buds, and stripes
    Of labdanum, and aloe-balls
Smeared with dull nard an Indian wipes
    From out her hair: (such balsam falls
    Down seaside mountain pedestals,
From summits where tired winds are fain,
Spent with the vast and howling main,
To treasure half their island-gain.)

And strew faint sweetness from some old
    Egyptian's fine worm-eaten shroud,
Which breaks to dust when once unrolled;
    And shred dim perfume, like a cloud
    From chamber long to quiet vowed,
With mothed and dropping arras hung,
Mouldering the lute and books among
Of queen, long dead, who lived there young.

"OVER THE SEA OUR GALLEYS WENT."

O VER the sea our galleys went,
  With cleaving prows in order brave,
To a speeding wind and a bounding wave,—
  A gallant armament:
Each bark built out of a forest-tree,
  Left leafy and rough as first it grew,
And nailed all over the gaping sides,
Within and without, with black-bull hides,
Seethed in fat and suppled in flame,
To bear the playful billows' game;
So each good ship was rude to see,
Rude and bare to the outward view,
  But each upbore a stately tent;
Where cedar-pales in scented row
Kept out the flakes of the dancing brine:
And an awning drooped the mast below,
In fold on fold of the purple fine,
That neither noontide, nor star-shine,

Nor moonlight cold which maketh mad,
   Might pierce the regal tenement.
When the sun dawned, O, gay **and** glad
We set the sail and plied the oar ;
But when the night-wind blew like breath,
For joy of one day's voyage more,
We sang together on the wide sea,
Like men **at peace on a** peaceful shore ;
Each sail was loosed to the wind so free,
Each helm made sure by the twilight star,
And in a sleep as calm as death,
We, **the** strangers from afar,
   Lay stretched along, each weary crew
In **a** circle round its wondrous tent,
Whence gleamed soft light and curled rich scent,
   And with light and perfume, music too :
So the stars wheeled round, and the darkness past,
And at morn we started beside the mast,
And still each **ship** was sailing **fast !**

One morn the land appeared ! — **a speck**
Dim trembling betwixt sea and **sky** —
Avoid it, cried our pilot, check
   The shout, restrain the longing eye !
But the heaving sea was black behind
For many a night and many a day,
And land, though but a rock, drew nigh ;
So we broke the cedar-pales away,
Let the purple awning flap in the wind,
   And a statue bright was on every deck !
We shouted, every man of us,
And steered right into the harbor thus,
With pomp and **pæan glorious.**

An hundred **shapes of lucid stone !**
   All day we built a shrine for **each** —
A shrine of rock for every one —
Nor paused we till in the westering sun
   We sate together on the beach

To sing, because our task was done;
When lo! what shouts and merry songs!
What laughter all the distance stirs!
What raft comes loaded with its throngs
Of gentle islanders?
" The isles are just at hand," they cried;
    "Like cloudlets faint at even sleeping,
Our temple-gates are opened wide,
    Our olive-groves thick shade are keeping
For the lucid shapes you bring,"—they cried.
O, then we awoke with sudden start
From our deep dream; we knew, too late,
How bare the rock, how desolate,
To which we had flung our precious freight:
    Yet we called out—"Depart!
Our gifts, once given, must here abide:
    Our work is done; we have no heart
To mar our work, though vain,"—we cried.

"ALL SERVICE RANKS THE SAME WITH GOD."

ALL service ranks the same with God:
    If now, as formerly He trod
Paradise, His presence fills
Our earth, each only as God wills
Can work,—God's puppets, best and worst,
Are we; there is no last nor first.

Say not "a small event"! Why "small"?
Costs it more pain than this, ye call
A "great event," should come to pass,
Than that? Untwine me from the mass
Of deeds which make up life, one deed
Power shall fall short in, or exceed!

"THE YEAR'S AT THE SPRING."

THE year's at the spring,
  And day's at the morn;
Morning's at seven;
The hillside's dew-pearled:
The lark's on the wing;
The snail's on the thorn;
God's in his heaven —
All's right with the world!

"A KING LIVED LONG AGO."

A KING lived long ago,
  In the morning of the world,
When earth was nigher heaven than now:
And the king's locks curled
Disparting o'er a forehead full
As the milk-white space 'twixt horn and horn
Of some sacrificial bull —
Only calm as a babe new-born:
For he was got to a sleepy mood,
So safe from all decrepitude,
From age with its bane so sure gone by,
(The Gods so loved him while he dreamed,)
That, having lived **thus** long, there seemed
No **need** the king should ever die.

Among the rocks his city was:
Before his palace, in the sun,
He sat to see his people pass,
And judge them every one
From its threshold of smooth stone.

They haled him many a valley-thief
Caught in the sheep-pens, — robber-chief,
Swarthy and shameless, — beggar cheat, —
Spy-prowler, — or rough pirate found
On the sea-sand left aground ;
And sometimes clung about his feet,
With bleeding lip and burning cheek,
A woman, bitterest wrong to speak
Of one with sullen thickset brows :
And sometimes from the prison-house
The angry priests a pale wretch brought,
Who through some chink had pushed and pressed,
On knees and elbows, belly and breast,
Worm-like into the temple, — caught
At last there by the very God,
Who ever in the darkness strode
Backward and forward, keeping watch
O'er his brazen bowls, such rogues to catch !
And these, all and every one,
The king judged, sitting in the sun.

His councillors, on left and right,
Looked anxious up, — but no surprise
Disturbed the king's old smiling eyes,
Where the very blue had turned to white.
'T is said, a Python scared one day
The breathless city, till he came,
With forky tongue and eyes on flame,
Where the old king sat to judge alway ;
But when he saw the sweepy hair,
Girt with a crown of berries rare
Which the God will hardly give to wear
To the maiden who singeth, dancing bare
In the altar-smoke by the pine-torch lights,
At his wondrous forest rites, —
Beholding this, he did not dare
Approach that threshold in the sun,
Assault the old king smiling there.
Such grace had kings when the world begun !

"YOU 'LL LOVE ME YET!"

YOU 'LL love me yet!— and I can tarry
    Your love's protracted growing :
June reared that bunch of flowers you carry
From seeds of April's sowing.

I plant a heartful now — some seed
    At least is sure to strike
And yield — what you 'll not pluck indeed,
    Not love, but, may be, like!

You 'll look at least on love's remains,
    A grave's one violet :
Your look? — That pays a thousand pains.
    What 's death? — You 'll love me yet!

"OVERHEAD THE TREE-TOPS MEET."

OVERHEAD the tree-tops meet—
    Flowers and grass spring 'neath one's feet —
There was naught above me, and naught below,
My childhood had not learned to know!
For, what are the voices of birds,
—Ay, and of beasts, — but words, — our words,
Only so much more sweet?
The knowledge of that with my life begun!
But I had so near made out the sun,
And counted your stars, the Seven and One,
Like the fingers of my hand :

Nay, I could all but understand
Wherefore through heaven the white moon ranges;
And just when out of her soft fifty changes
No unfamiliar face might overlook me —
Suddenly God took me!

MARCHING ALONG.

KENTISH Sir Byng stood for his King,
 Bidding the crop-headed Parliament swing:
And, pressing a troop unable to stoop
And see the rogues flourish and honest folk droop,
Marched them along, fifty-score strong,
Great-hearted gentlemen, singing this song.

God for King Charles! Pym and such carles
To the Devil that prompts 'em their treasonous parles!
Cavaliers, up! Lips from the cup,
Hands from the pasty, nor bite take nor sup
Till you 're (*Chorus*) marching along, fifty-score strong,
Great-hearted gentlemen, singing this song.

Hampden to Hell, and his obsequies' knell
Serve Hazelrig, Fiennes, and young Harry as well!
England, good cheer! Rupert is near!
Kentish and loyalists, keep we not here
          (*Cho.*) Marching along, fifty-score strong,
              Great-hearted gentlemen, singing this song?

Then, God for King Charles! Pym and his snarls
To the Devil that pricks on such pestilent carles!
Hold by the right, you double your might;
So, onward to Nottingham, fresh for the fight,
          (*Cho.*) March we along, fifty-score strong,
              Great-hearted gentlemen, singing this song.

GIVE A ROUSE.

KING CHARLES, and who 'll do him right now?
King Charles, and who 's ripe for fight now?
Give a rouse: here 's, in Hell's despite now,
King Charles!

Who gave me the goods that went since?
Who raised me the house that sank once?
Who helped me to gold I spent since?
Who found me in wine you drank once?
        (*Cho.*) King Charles, and who 'll do him right now?
               King Charles, and who 's ripe for fight now?
               Give a rouse: here 's, in Hell's despite now,
               King Charles!

To whom used my boy George quaff else,
By the old fool's side that begot him?
For whom did he cheer and laugh else,
While Noll's damned troopers shot him?
        (*Cho.*) King Charles, and who 'll do him right now?
               King Charles, and who 's ripe for fight now?
               Give a rouse: here 's, in Hell's despite now,
               King Charles!

BOOT AND SADDLE.

BOOT, saddle, to horse, and away!
   Rescue my Castle, before the hot day
Brightens to blue from its silvery gray,
       (*Cho.*) **Boot**, saddle, to horse, and away!

Ride past the suburbs, **asleep as** you 'd say;
Many 's the friend there will listen and pray
"**God's luck to gallants** that strike up the lay,
       (*Cho.*) **Boot, saddle,** to horse, and away!"

Forty miles off, **like a roebuck at bay,**
Flouts Castle Brancepeth **the Roundheads'** array:
Who laughs, "Good fellows **ere this, by** my fay,
       (*Cho.*) Boot, saddle, to horse, and **away?**"

Who?   My wife Gertrude; that, honest and gay,
Laughs when you talk of surrendering, "Nay!
I 've better counsellors; what counsel they?
       (*Cho.*) Boot, saddle, to horse, and away!"

"THERE 'S A WOMAN LIKE·A DEW–DROP."

THERE 'S a woman like a dew-drop, she 's so purer than the
      purest ;
And her noble heart 's the noblest, yes, and her sure faith 's the
      surest :
And her eyes are dark and humid, like the depth on depth of lustre
Hid i' the harebell, while her tresses, sunnier than the wild-grape
      cluster,
Gush in golden-tinted plenty down her neck's rose-misted marble :
Then her voice's music . . . call it the well's bubbling, the bird's
      warble !

And this woman says, "My days were sunless and my nights
 were moonless,
Parched the pleasant April herbage, and the lark's heart's out-
 break tuneless,
If you loved me not!" And I who, — (ah, for words of flame!)
 adore her!
Who am mad to lay my spirit prostrate palpably before her, —
I may enter at her portal soon, as now her lattice takes me,
And by noontide as by midnight make her mine, as hers she
 makes me!

MY LAST DUCHESS.

THAT 'S my last Duchess painted on the wall,
 Looking as if she were alive; I call
That piece a wonder, now: Frà Pandolf's hands
Worked busily a day, and there she stands.
Will 't please you sit and look at her?   I said
"Frà Pandolf" by design, for never read
Strangers like you that pictured countenance,
The depth and passion of its earnest glance,
But to myself they turned (since none puts by
The curtain I have drawn for you, but I)
And seemed as they would ask me, if they durst,
How such a glance came there; so, not the first
Are you to turn and ask thus.   Sir, 't was not
Her husband's presence only, called that spot
Of joy into the Duchess' cheek: perhaps
Frà Pandolf chanced to say "Her mantle laps
Over my Lady's wrist too much," or "Paint
Must never hope to reproduce the faint
Half-flush that dies along her throat"; such stuff
Was courtesy, she thought, and cause enough
For calling up that spot of joy.   She had

A heart . . . **how shall** I say ? . . . too soon made glad,
Too easily impressed; she liked whate'er
She looked on, and her looks went everywhere.
Sir, 't was all one!   My favor at her breast,
The dropping of the daylight in the West,
The bough of cherries some officious fool
Broke in the orchard for her, the white mule
She rode with round the terrace, — all and each
Would draw from her alike the approving speech,
Or blush, at least.   She thanked men, — good ; but thanked
Somehow . . . I know not how . . . **as** if she ranked
My gift of a nine hundred years old name
With anybody's gift.   Who 'd stoop to blame
This sort of trifling ?   Even had you skill
In speech — (which I have not) — to make your **will**
Qnite clear to such an one, and say "Just this
Or that in you disgusts me ; here you miss,
Or there exceed the mark" — and if she let
Herself be lessoned so, nor plainly set
Her wits to yours, forsooth, and made excuse,
— E'en then **would be** some stooping, and I chuse
Never to stoop.   O, Sir, she smiled, no doubt,
Whene'er I passed her ; but who passed without
Much the same smile ?   This grew ; I gave commands ;
Then all smiles stopped together.   There she stands
As if alive.   Will 't please you rise ?   We 'll **meet**
The company below, then.   I repeat,
The Count your Master's known munificence
Is **ample** warrant that no just pretence
Of **mine** for dowry will be disallowed ;
Though his fair daughter's self, as I avowed
At starting, is my object.   Nay, we 'll go
Together down, Sir !   Notice Neptune, though,
Taming a sea-horse, thought a rarity,
Which Claus of Innsbruck cast in bronze for me.

SOLILOQUY OF THE SPANISH CLOISTER.

G R-R-R — there go, my heart's abhorrence!
   Water your damned flower-pots, do!
If hate killed men, Brother Lawrence,
   God's blood, would not mine kill you!
What? your myrtle-bush wants trimming?
   O, that rose has prior claims, —
Needs its leaden vase filled brimming?
   Hell dry you up with its flames!

At the meal we sit together:
   Salve tibi! I must hear
Wise talk of the kind of weather,
   Sort of season, time of year:
Not a plenteous cork-crop: scarcely
   Dare we hope oak-galls, I doubt:
What's the Latin name for "parsley"?
   What's the Greek name for Swine's Snout?

Whew! We'll have our platter burnished,
   Laid with care on our own shelf!
With a fire-new spoon we're furnished,
   And a goblet for ourself,
Rinsed like something sacrificial
   Ere 't is fit to touch our chaps, —
Marked with L. for our initial!
   (He, he! There his lily snaps!)

Saint, forsooth! While brown Dolores
   Squats outside the Convent bank,
With Sanchicha, telling stories,
   Steeping tresses in the tank,
Blue-black, lustrous, thick like horse-hairs,
   — Can't I see his dead eye glow

Bright, as 't were a Barbary corsair's?
(That is, if he 'd let it show!)

When he finishes refection,
    Knife and fork he never lays
Cross-wise, to my recollection,
    As do I, in Jesu's praise.
I, the Trinity illustrate,
    Drinking watered orange-pulp, —
In three sips the Arian frustrate;
    While he drains his at one gulp!

O, those melons! If he 's able
    We 're to have a feast; so nice!
One goes to the Abbot's table,
    All of us get each a slice.
How go on your flowers? None double?
    Not one fruit-sort can you spy?
Strange! — And I, too, at such trouble,
    Keep 'em close-nipped on the sly!

There 's a great text in Galatians,
    Once you trip on it, entails
Twenty-nine distinct damnations,
    One sure, if another fails.
If I trip him just a-dying,
    Sure of Heaven as sure can be,
Spin him round and send him flying
    Off to Hell, a Manichee!

Or, my scrofulous French novel,
    On gray paper with blunt type!
Simply glance at it, you grovel
    Hand and foot in Belial's gripe:
If I double down its pages
    At the woful sixteenth point,
When he gathers his greengages,
    Ope a sieve and slip it in 't!

Or, there 's **Satan !** — one might venture
  Pledge one's soul to him, yet leave
Such a flaw in the indenture
  As he 'd miss till, past retrieve,
Blasted lay that rose-acacia
  We 're so proud of ! *Hy, Zy, Hine* . .
'**St,** there 's Vespers ! *Plena gratiâ*
  Ave Virgo ! Gr-r-r — you swine !

THROUGH THE METIDJA TO ABD-EL-KADR.

A S I ride, as I ride,
    With a full **heart for my guide,**
So its tide rocks **my side,**
As I ride, as I ride,
That, **as I were** double-eyed,
He, in whom our Tribes confide,
Is descried, ways untried
As I ride, as I ride.

As I ride, as I ride
To our Chief and his Allied,
Who dares chide my **heart's pride**
As I ride, as I ride ?
Or are witnesses denied, —
Through the desert waste and wide
Do I glide unespied
As I ride, as I ride ?

As I ride, as I ride,
When an inner voice has cried,
The sands slide, nor abide
(As I ride, as I ride)

O'er each visioned Homicide
That came vaunting (has he lied?)
To reside — where he died,
As I ride, **as** I ride.

As I ride, as **I** ride,
Ne'er has spur my **swift horse plied,**
Yet his hide, streaked and pied,
As I ride, as I ride,
Shows where sweat has sprung and dried,
— Zebra-footed, ostrich-thighed, —
How has vied stride with **stride**
As I ride, as I ride!

As I ride, as I ride,
Could I loose what Fate has **tied,**
Ere I pried, she should hide
As I ride, as **I ride,**
All that's meant me : satisfied
When the Prophet and the **Bride**
Stop veins I'd have subside
As I ride, as I ride!

COUNT GISMOND.

CHRIST God, who savest men, save most
   Of men Count Gismond who saved me!
Count Gauthier, **when he** chose his post,
  Chose time and place and company
To suit it; when he struck at length
My honor 't was with all his strength.

And doubtlessly ere he could draw
  All points to one, he must have schemed.

That miserable morning saw
  Few half so happy as I seemed,
While being dressed in Queen's array
To give our Tourney prize away.

I thought they loved me, did me grace
  To please themselves; 't was all their deed:
God makes, or fair or foul, our face;
  If showing mine so caused to bleed
My cousins' hearts, they should have dropped
A word, and straight the play had stopped.

They, too, so beauteous! Each a queen
  By virtue of her brow and breast;
Not needing to be crowned, I mean,
  As I do. E'en when I was dressed,
Had either of them spoke, instead
Of glancing sideways with still head!

But no: they let me laugh, and sing
  My birthday song quite through, adjust
The last rose in my garland, fling
  A last look on the mirror, trust
My arms to each an arm of theirs,
And so descend the castle-stairs, —

And come out on the morning troop
  Of merry friends who kissed my cheek,
And called me Queen, and made me stoop
  Under the canopy, — (a streak
That pierced it, of the outside sun,
Powdered with gold its gloom's soft dun,) —

And they could let me take my state
  And foolish throne amid applause
Of all come there to celebrate
  My Queen's day, — O, I think the cause
Of much was, they forgot no crowd
Makes up for parents in their shroud!

Howe'er that be, all eyes were bent
  Upon me, when my cousins cast
Theirs down; 't was time I should present
  The victor's crown, but . . . there, 't will **last**
No long time . . . the old mist again
Blinds me **as then** it did.   How vain!

See! Gismond 's at the gate, in talk
  With his two boys : I can proceed.
Well, at that moment, who should stalk
  Forth boldly (to my face, indeed)
But Gauthier, and he thundered " Stay ! "
And all stayed.   "Bring no crowns, I say ! "

" Bring torches!   Wind the penance-sheet
  About her !   Let her shun the chaste,
Or lay herself before their feet !
  Shall she, whose body I embraced
A night long, **queen it** in the **day** ?
For Honor's **sake no crowns, I say ! "**

I?   What I answered ?   As **I live**
  I never fancied such a thing
As answer possible to give.
  What says the body when they spring
Some monstrous torture-engine's whole
Strength on it ?   No **more** says the soul.

Till out strode Gismond ; **then I knew**
  That I was saved.   **I never met**
His face before, but, at first view,
  I felt quite **sure** that God had set
Himself **to Satan ;** who would spend
A minute's **mistrust on** the end ?

He **strode to Gauthier,** in his throat
  Gave him the lie, then struck his mouth
With one back-handed blow that wrote
  In blood men's verdict there.   North, South,

East, **West, I looked.** The lie was dead,
And damned, and truth stood up instead.

This glads me most, that I enjoyed
   The heart of the joy, with my content
In watching Gismond unalloyed
   By any doubt of the event:
God took that on him, — I was bid
Watch Gismond for my part: I did.

Did I not watch him while he let
   His armorer just brace his greaves,
Rivet his hauberk, on the fret
   The while! His foot . . . **my** memory leaves
No least stamp out, nor how **anon**
He pulled his **ringing gauntlets on.**

And e'en before **the trumpet's** sound
   Was finished, prone lay the false Knight,
Prone as his lie upon the ground:
   Gismond flew at him, used no sleight
Of the sword, but open-breasted drove,
Cleaving till out the truth he clove.

Which done, he dragged him to my feet
   And said, " Here die, but end thy breath
In full confession, lest thou fleet
   From **my** first, to God's second death!
Say hast **thou** lied ? " And " I have lied
To God **and her,**" he said, and died.

Then Gismond, kneeling to me, asked
   — What safe my heart holds, **though no word**
Could I repeat now, if I tasked
   My powers forever, to a third
Dear even as you are. Pass the rest
Until I sank upon his breast.

Over my head his arm he flung
   Against the world; and scarce **I felt**

His sword, that dripped by me and swung,
  A little shifted in its belt, —
For he began to say the while
How South our home lay many a mile.

So 'mid the shouting multitude
  We two walked forth to never more
Return. My cousins have pursued
  Their life, untroubled as before

    3

I vexed them.   Gauthier's dwelling-place
God lighten!   May his soul find grace!

Our elder boy has got the clear
   Great brow; tho' when his brother's black
Full eye shows scorn, it . . . Gismond here?
   And have you brought my tercel back?
I just was telling Adela
How many birds it struck since May.

THE LOST LEADER.

JUST for a handful of silver he left us,
   Just for a ribbon to stick in his coat, —
Found the one gift of which fortune bereft us,
   Lost all the others she lets us devote;
They, with the gold to give, doled him out silver,
   So much was their's who so little allowed:
How all our copper had gone for his service!
   Rags, — were they purple, his heart had been proud!
We that had loved him so, followed him, honored him,
   Lived in his mild and magnificent eye,
Learned his great language, caught his clear accents,
   Made him our pattern to live and to die!
Shakespeare was of us, Milton was for us,
   Burns, Shelley, were with us, — they watch from their graves!
He alone breaks from the van and the freemen,
   He alone sinks to the rear and the slaves!

We shall march prospering, — not through his presence;
   Songs may inspirit us, — not from his lyre;
Deeds will be done, — while he boasts his quiescence,
   Still bidding crouch whom the rest bade aspire:

Blot out his name, then, — record one lost soul more,
   One task more declined, one more footpath untrod,
One more triumph for devils, and sorrow for angels,
   One wrong more to man, one more insult to God!
Life's night begins: let him never come back to us!
   There would be doubt, hesitation, and pain,
Forced praise on our part, the glimmer of twilight,
   Never glad confident morning again!
Best fight on well, for we taught him, — strike gallantly,
   Aim at our heart ere we pierce through his own;
Then let him receive the new knowledge and wait us,
   Pardoned in Heaven, the first by the throne!

THE LOST MISTRESS.

ALL'S over, then, — does truth sound bitter
   As one at first believes?
Hark, 't is the sparrows' good-night twitter
   About your cottage eaves!

And the leaf-buds on the vine are woolly,
   I noticed that, to-day;
One day more bursts them open fully,
   — You know the red turns gray.

To-morrow we meet the same then, dearest?
   May I take your hand in mine?
Mere friends are we, — well, friends the merest
   Keep much that I 'll resign:

For each glance of that eye so bright and black,
   Though I keep with heart's endeavor, —
Your voice, when you wish the snowdrops back,
   Though it stays in my soul forever! —

— Yet I will but say what mere friends say,
  Or only a thought stronger;
I will hold your hand but as long as **all may,**
  Or so very little longer!

HOME THOUGHTS, FROM ABROAD.

OH, to be in England
  Now that April's there,
And whoever wakes in England
Sees, some morning, unaware,
That the **lowest** boughs and **the** brushwood **sheaf**
Round the elm-tree bole are **in** tiny leaf,
While the chaffinch **sings on** the orchard **bough**
In England — **now**!

  And after April, when May follows,
And the white-throat builds, and all the swallows, —
Hark! where my blossomed pear-tree in the hedge
Leans to the field and scatters **on** the clover
Blossoms and dewdrops, — **at the** bent spray's edge, —
That's the wise thrush; **he sings** each song twice over,
Lest you should think he **never** could recapture
The first fine, **careless** rapture!
And though the fields look rough with hoary dew,
All will be gay when noontide wakes anew
The buttercups, the little children's dower,
— Far brighter than this gaudy melon-flower!

HOME THOUGHTS, FROM THE SEA.

N OBLY, nobly Cape Saint Vincent to the northwest died
　　away ;
Sunset ran, one glorious blood-red, reeking into Cadiz Bay ;
Bluish mid the burning water, full in face Trafalgar lay ;
In the dimmest northeast distance, dawned Gibraltar grand and
　　gray ;
" Here and here did England help me, — how can I help Eng-
　　land ? " — say,
Whoso turns as I, this evening, turn to God to praise and pray,
While Jove's planet rises yonder, silent over Africa.

THE FLOWER'S NAME.

H ERE 'S the garden she walked across,
　　Arm in my arm, such a short while since :
Hark, now I push its wicket, the moss
　　Hinders the hinges and makes them wince !
She must have reached this shrub ere she turned,
　　As back with that murmur the wicket swung ;
For she laid the poor snail, my chance foot spurned,
　　To feed and forget it the leaves among.

Down this side of the gravel-walk
　　She went while her robe's edge brushed the box :
And here she paused in her gracious talk
　　To point me a moth on the milk-white flox.
Roses, ranged in valiant row,
　　I will never think that she passed you by !
She loves you noble roses, I know ;
　　But yonder see, where the rock-plants lie !

This flower she stopped at, finger on lip,
   Stooped over, in doubt, as settling its claim ;
Till she gave me, with pride to make no slip,
   Its soft meandering Spanish name.
What a name !   Was it love, or praise ?
   Speech half-asleep, or song half-awake ?
I must learn Spanish, one of these days,
   Only for that slow, sweet name's sake.

Roses, if I live and do well,
   I may bring her, one of these days,
To fix you fast with as fine a spell,
   Fit you each with his Spanish phrase !
But do not detain me now ; for she lingers
   There, like sunshine over the ground,
And ever I see her soft white fingers
   Searching after the bud she found.

Flower, you Spaniard, look that you grow not,
   Stay as you are and be loved forever !
Bud, if I kiss you 't is that you blow not,
   Mind, the shut pink mouth opens never !
For while thus it pouts, her fingers wrestle,
   Twinkling the audacious leaves between,
Till round they turn and down they nestle, —
   Is not the dear mark still to be seen ?

Where I find her not, beauties vanish ;
   Whither I follow her, beauties flee ;
Is there no method to tell her in Spanish
   June's twice June since she breathed it with me ?
Come, bud, show me the least of her traces,
   Treasure my lady's lightest footfall
—Ah, you may flout and turn up your faces, —
   Roses, you are not so fair after all !

THE PIED PIPER OF HAMELIN.

HAMELIN Town 's in Brunswick,
  By famous Hanover city ;
The river Weser, deep and wide,
Washes its wall on the southern side ;
A pleasanter spot you never spied ;
But, when begins my ditty,
  Almost five hundred years ago,
  To see the townsfolk suffer so
    From vermin, was a pity.

  Rats !
They fought the dogs, and killed the cats,
  And bit the babies in the cradles,
And ate the cheeses out of the vats,
  And licked the soup from the cook's own ladles,
Split open the kegs of salted sprats,
Made nests inside men's Sunday hats,
And even spoiled the women's chats,
    By drowning their speaking
    With shrieking and squeaking
In fifty different sharps and flats.

At last the people in a body
  To the Town Hall came flocking :
" 'T is clear," cried they, " our Mayor 's a noddy ;
  And as for our Corporation, — shocking
To think we buy gowns lined with ermine
For dolts that can't or won't determine
What 's best to rid us of our vermin !
You hope, because you 're old and obese,
To find in the furry civic robe ease ?
Rouse up, Sirs ! Give your brains a racking
To find the remedy we 're lacking,
Or, sure as fate, we 'll send you packing ! "

At this the Mayor and Corporation
Quaked with a mighty consternation.

An hour they sat in counsel,
   At length the Mayor broke silence :
" For a guilder I 'd my ermine gown sell ;
   I wish I were a mile hence !
It 's easy to bid one rack one's brain, —
I 'm sure my poor head aches again
I 've scratched it so, and all in vain.
O for a trap, a trap, a trap ! "
Just as he said this, what should hap
At the chamber door but a gentle tap ?
" Bless us," cried the Mayor, " what 's that ? "
(With the Corporation as he sat,
Looking little, though wondrous fat ;
Nor brighter was his eye, nor moister
Than a too long-opened oyster,
Save when at noon his paunch grew mutinous
For a plate of turtle green and glutinous)
" Only a scraping of shoes on the mat ?
Anything like the sound of a rat
Makes my heart go pit-a-pat ! "

" Come in ! " — the Mayor cried, looking bigger :
And in did come the strangest figure !
His queer long coat from heel to head
Was half of yellow and half of red ;
And he himself was tall and thin,
With sharp blue eyes, each like a pin,
And light loose hair, yet swarthy skin,
No tuft on cheek nor beard on chin,
But lips where smiles went out and in, —
There was no guessing his kith and kin !
And nobody could enough admire
The tall man and his quaint attire :
Quoth one : " It 's as my great-grandsire,
Starting up at the Trump of Doom's tone,
Had walked this way from his painted tomb-stone ! "

He advanced to the council-table :
And, " Please your honors," said he, " I 'm able,
By means of a secret charm, to draw
All creatures living beneath the sun,
That creep, or swim, or fly, or run,
After me so as you never saw !
And I chiefly use my charm
On creatures that do people harm,
The mole, and toad, and newt, and viper ;
And people call me the Pied Piper."
(And here they noticed round his neck
A scarf of red and yellow stripe,
To match with his coat of the selfsame check ;
And at the scarf's end hung a pipe ;
And his fingers, they noticed, were ever straying
As if impatient to be playing
Upon this pipe, as low it dangled
Over his vesture so old-fangled.)
" Yet," said he, " poor piper as I am,
In Tartary I freed the Cham
Last June from his huge swarms of gnats ;
I eased in Asia the Nizam
Of a monstrous brood of vampyre-bats :
And, as for what your brain bewilders,
If I can rid your town of rats
Will you give me a thousand guilders ?"
" One ? fifty thousand ! " — was the exclamation
Of the astonished Mayor and Corporation.

Into the street the Piper stept,
    Smiling first a little smile,
As if he new what magic slept
    In his quiet pipe the while ;
Then, like a musical adept,
To blow the pipe his lips he wrinkled,
And green and blue his sharp eyes twinkled
Like a candle flame where salt is sprinkled ;
And ere three shrill notes the pipe uttered,
You heard as if an army muttered ;

And the muttering grew to a grumbling;
And the grumbling grew to a mighty rumbling,
And out of the houses the rats came tumbling.
Great rats, small rats, lean rats, brawny rats,
Brown rats, black rats, gray rats, tawny rats,
Grave old plodders, gay young friskers,
  'Fathers, mothers, uncles, cousins,

Cocking tails and pricking whiskers,
  Families by tens and dozens,
Brothers, sisters, husbands, wives —
Followed the Piper for their lives.
From street to street he piped advancing,
And step for step they followed dancing,
Until they came to the river Weser
Wherein all plunged and perished,
— Save one who, stout as Julius Cæsar,
Swam across and lived to carry
(As he the manuscript he cherished)
To Rat-land home his commentary,
Which was, " At the first shrill notes of the pipe,
I heard a sound as of scraping tripe,
And putting apples, wondrous ripe,
Into a cider-press's gripe :
And a moving away of pickle-tub-boards,
And a leaving ajar of conserve-cupboards,
And a drawing the corks of train-oil-flasks,
And a breaking the hoops of butter-casks ;
And it seemed as if a voice
(Sweeter far than by harp or by psaltery
Is breathed) called out, O rats, rejoice !
The world is grown to one vast drysaltery !
So munch on, crunch on, take your nuncheon,
Breakfast, supper, dinner, luncheon !
And just as a bulky sugar-puncheon,
All ready staved, like a great sun shone
Glorious scarce an inch before me,
Just as methought it said, Come, bore me !
— I found the Weser rolling o'er me."

You should have heard the Hamelin people
Ringing the bells till they rocked the steeple ;
" Go," cried the Mayor, " and get long poles !
Poke out the nests and block up the holes !
Consult with carpenters and builders,
And leave in our town nót even a trace
Of the rats ! " — when suddenly up the face

Of the Piper perked in the market-place,
With a, " First if you please, my thousand guilders ! "

A thousand guilders !   The Mayor looked blue ;
So did the Corporation too.
For council dinners made rare havock
With Claret, Moselle, Vin-de-Grave, Hock ;
And half the money would replenish
Their cellar's biggest butt with Rhenish.
To pay this sum to a wandering fellow
With a gypsy coat of red and yellow !
" Beside," quoth the Mayor with a knowing wink,
" Our business was done at the river's brink ;
We saw with our eyes the vermin sink,
And what 's dead can't come to life I think.
So, friend, we 're not the folks to shrink
From the duty of giving you something for drink,
And a matter of money to put in your poke ;
But, as for the guilders, what we spoke
Of them, as you very well know, was in joke.
Beside, our losses have made us thrifty ;
A thousand guilders !   Come, take fifty ! "

The Piper's face fell, and he cried,
" No trifling !   I can't wait, beside !
I 've promised to visit by dinner time
Bagdat, and accept the prime
Of the Head Cook's pottage, all he 's rich in,
For having left, in the Caliph's kitchen,
Of a nest of scorpions no survivor, —
With him I proved no bargain-driver,
With you, don't think I 'll bate a stiver !
And folks who put me in a passion
May find me pipe to another fashion."

" How ? " cried the Mayor, " d' ye think I 'll brook
Being worse treated than a Cook ?
Insulted by a lazy ribald
With idle pipe and vesture piebald ?

You threaten us, fellow?   Do your worst,
Blow your pipe there till you burst!"

Once more he stept into the street;
  And to his lips again
Laid his long pipe of **smooth** straight **cane;**
  And ere he blew three notes (such **sweet**
Soft notes as yet musician's cunning
  Never gave the enraptured air)
There was a rustling, that seemed **like a** bustling
Of merry crowds justling at pitching and hustling,
Small feet were pattering, wooden shoes clattering,
Little hands clapping, and little tongues chattering,
And, **like** fowls in a farm-yard when barley is scattering,
Out came the children running.
All the little boys and girls,
With rosy cheeks and flaxen curls,
And sparkling eyes and teeth like pearls,
Tripping and skipping, ran merrily after
The wonderful **music** with shouting and laughter.

The Mayor was dumb, and the Council stood
As **if** they were **changed into blocks of wood,**
Unable to move a step, or cry
To the children merrily skipping by, —
And could **only** follow with the eye
That joyous crowd at the Piper's back.
But how the Mayor was on the rack,
And the wretched Council's bosoms beat,
As the Piper turned from the High **Street**
To where the Weser rolled **its waters**
Right **in the way of** their sons and daughters!
However he **turned from South** to West,
And **to** Koppelberg Hill his steps addressed,
And **after** him the children pressed;
Great **was the** joy in every breast.
" He never can cross that mighty top!
He 's forced to **let the** piping drop,
And we shall see our children stop!"

When, lo! as they reached the **mountain's side,**
A wondrous portal opened wide,
As if a cavern was suddenly hollowed;
And the Piper advanced and the children followed,
And when all were in to the very last,
The door in the mountain side shut fast.
Did I say all? No. One was lame,
And could not dance the whole of the way;
And in after years, if you would blame
His sadness, he was used to say, —
"It's dull in our town since my playmates **left!**
I can't forget that I'm bereft
Of **all** the pleasant sights **they see,**
Which the Piper also promised me;
For he led **us,** he said, to a joyous land,
Joining the town **and** just at hand,
Where waters gushed and fruit-trees grew,
And flowers put forth **a fairer hue,**
And everything was strange and **new;**
The sparrows were brighter than **peacocks here,**
And their dogs outran our fallow **deer,**
And honey-bees had lost their stings,
And horses were born with eagles' wings;
And just as I became assured
My lame foot would be speedily cured,
The music stopped and I stood still,
And found myself outside the Hill,
Left alone against my will,
To go now limping as before,
And never hear of **that** country more!"

Alas! **alas for Hamelin!**
    There came into many a burgher's pate
    A text which says, that Heaven's Gate
    Opes to the Rich at as easy rate
As the needle's eye takes a camel in!
The Mayor sent East, West, North, **and South**
To offer the Piper by word of mouth,
    Wherever it was men's lot to find him,
Silver and gold to his heart's content,

If he 'd only return the way he went,
  And bring the children behind him.
But when they saw 't was a lost endeavor,
And Piper and dancers were gone forever,
They made a decree that lawyers never
  Should think their records dated duly
If, after the day of the month and year,
These words did not as well appear,
" And so long after what happened here
  On the Twenty-second of Júly,
Thirteen hundred and Seventy-six " :
And the better in memory to fix
The place of the Children's last retreat,
They called it, the Pied Piper's Street, —
Where any one playing on pipe or tabor
Was sure for the future to lose his labor.
Nor suffered they Hostelry or Tavern
  To shock with mirth a street so solemn ;
But opposite the place of the cavern
  They wrote the story on a column,
And on the Great Church Window painted
The same, to make the world acquainted
How their children were stolen away ;
And there it stands to this very day.
And I must not omit to say
That in Transylvania there 's a tribe
Of alien people that ascribe
The outlandish ways and dress
On which their neighbors lay such stress,
To their fathers and mothers having risen
Out of some subterraneous prison
Into which they were trepanned
Long time ago in a mighty band
Out of Hamelin town in Brunswick land,
But how or why, they don't understand.

So, Willy, let you and me be wipers
Of scores out with all men — especially pipers :
And, whether they pipe us free from rats or fróm mice,
If we 've promised them aught, let us keep our promise.

FAME.

SEE, as the prettiest graves will do in time,
    Our poet's wants the freshness of its prime;
Spite of the sexton's browsing horse, the sods
Have struggled through its binding osier-rods;
Headstone and half-sunk footstone lean awry,
Wanting the brickwork promised by and by;
How the minute gray lichens, plate o'er plate,
Have softened down the crisp-cut name and date!

LOVE.

SO, the year 's done with!
        (*Love me forever!*)
All March begun with,
    April's endeavor;
May-wreaths that bound me
    June needs must sever!
Now snows fall round me,
    Quenching June's fever, —
        (*Love me forever!*)

SONG.

NAY but you, who do not love her,
    Is she not pure gold, my mistress?
Holds earth aught, — speak truth, — above her?
    Aught like this tress, see, and this tress,

And this last fairest tress of all
So fair, see, ere I let it fall!

Because, you spend your lives in praising;
   To praise, you search the wide world over;
So, why not witness, calmly gazing,
   If earth holds aught — speak truth — above her?
Above this tress, and this I touch
But cannot praise, I love so much!

INCIDENT OF THE FRENCH CAMP.

YOU know, we French stormed Ratisbon:
   A mile or so away
On a little mound, Napoléon
   Stood on our storming-day;
With neck out-thrust, you fancy how, •
   Legs wide, arms locked behind,
As if to balance the prone brow
   Oppressive with its mind.

Just as perhaps he mused, "My plans
   That soar, to earth may fall,
Let once my army-leader, Lannes,
   Waver at yonder wall," —
Out 'twixt the battery-smokes there flew
   A rider, bound on bound
Full-galloping; nor bridle drew
   Until he reached the mound.

Then off there flung in smiling joy,
   And held himself erect
By just his horse's mane, a boy:
   You hardly could suspect —

4 •

(So tight he kept his lips compressed,
  Scarce any blood came through)
You looked twice ere you saw his breast
  Was all but shot in two.

" Well," cried he, " Emperor, by God's grace
  We 've got you Ratisbon !
The Marshal 's in the market-place,
  And you 'll be there anon

To see your flag-bird flap his vans
  Where I, to heart's desire,
Perched him!" The Chief's eye flashed; his plans
  Soared up again like fire.

The Chief's eye flashed; but presently
  Softened itself, as sheathes
A film the mother eagle's eye
  When her bruised eaglet breathes:
" You 're wounded!" "Nay," his soldier's pride
  Touched to the quick, he said:
" I 'm killed, Sire!" And, his Chief beside,
  Smiling, the boy fell dead.

THE BOY AND THE ANGEL.

MORNING, evening, noon, and night,
  " Praise God," sang Theocrite.

Then to his poor trade he turned,
By which the daily meal was earned.

Hard he labored, long and well;
O'er his work the boy's curls fell:

But ever, at each period,
He stopped and sang, " Praise God."

Then back again his curls he threw,
And cheerful turned to work anew.

Said Blaise, the listening monk, " Well done;
I doubt not thou art heard, my son:

" As well as if thy voice to-day
Were praising God, the Pope's great way.

" This Easter Day, the Pope at Rome
Praises God from Peter's dome."

Said Theocrite, " Would God that I
Might praise Him, that great way, and die ! "

Night passed, day shone,
And Theocrite was gone.

With God a day endures alway,
A thousand years are but a day.

God said in Heaven, " Nor day nor night
Now brings the voice of my delight."

Then Gabriel, like a rainbow's birth,
Spread his wings and sank to earth ;

Entered in flesh, the empty cell,
Lived there, and played the craftsman well :

And morning, evening, noon, and night,
Praised God in place of Theocrite.

And from a boy, to youth he grew :
The man put off the stripling's hue :

The man matured and fell away
Into the season of decay :

And ever o'er the trade he bent,
And ever lived on earth content.

(He did God's will ; to him, all one
If on the earth or in the sun.)

God said, " A praise is in mine ear ;
There is no doubt in it, no fear :

" So sing old worlds, and so
New worlds that from my footstool go.

" Clearer loves sound other ways :
I miss my little human praise."

Then **forth** sprang Gabriel's wings, off fell
The **flesh** disguise, remained the cell.

'T was **Easter Day** : he flew **to** Rome,
And **paused** above Saint Peter's **dome.**

In the tiring-room close **by**
The **great** outer gallery,

With his holy vestments dight,
Stood the new Pope, **Theocrite**

And all **his past career**
Came **back upon him clear,**

Since when, **a boy,** he plied his trade,
Till on **his life the** sickness weighed ;

And in his cell, when death drew near,
An **angel** in a dream brought **cheer ;**

And rising from the sickness **drear**
He **grew** a priest, and now **stood here.**

To the **East** with praise he **turned,**
And **on** his sight the angel **burned.**

" I bore thee from thy craftsman's cell,
And set thee here ; I did not well.

" Vainly I left my angel's-sphere,
Vain was thy dream of many a year.

" Thy **voice's praise** seemed weak ; it dropped, —
Creation's chorus stopped !

" Go back and praise again
The early way, — while **I remain.**

" With that weak voice of our disdain,
Take up Creation's pausing strain.

" **Back** to the cell and poor employ:
Become the craftsman and the boy ! "

Theocrite **grew old** at home ;
A new Pope dwelt in Peter's Dome.

One vanished as the other died :
They sought God side by **side.**

TIME'S REVENGES.

I 'VE a Friend, over the sea ;
 I like him, but he loves me ;
It all grew out of the books I write ;
They find such favor in his sight
That he slaughters you with savage looks
Because you don't admire my books :
He does himself though, — and if **some vein**
Were to snap to-night in this heavy **brain,**
To-morrow month, if I lived to **try,**
Round should I just turn quietly,
Or out of the bedclothes stretch my hand
Till **I found him, come from** his foreign land
To be my nurse in this poor place,
And make me broth and wash my face,
And light my fire, and, all the while,
Bear with his old good-humored smile
That I told him, " Better have kept away

Than come and kill me, night and day,
With worse than fever's throbs and shoots,
At the creaking of his clumsy boots."
I am as sure that this he would do,
As that St. Paul's is striking Two :
And I think I had rather . . . woe is **me**
— Yes, rather see him than not see,
If lifting a hand would seat him there
Before me in the empty chair
To-night, when my head aches **indeed**,
And I can neither think, nor read,
And these blue fingers will not hold
The pen ; this garret 's freezing cold!

And I 've a Lady — There he wakes,
The laughing fiend and prince of snakes
Within me, at her name, **to** pray
Fate send some creature in the **way**
Of my love for her, to be down-torn,
Upthrust **and onward** borne
So I might prove myself that sea
Of passion **which I** needs must be!
Call my thoughts false and my fancies quaint,
And my style infirm, and its figures faint,
All the critics say, and more blame yet,
And not one angry word you get!
But, please you, wonder I would put
My cheek beneath that Lady's foot
Rather than trample under mine
The laurels of the Florentine,
And you shall see how the Devil spends
A fire God gave for other ends!
I tell you, I stride up and down
This garret, crowned with love's best **crown**,
And feasted with love's perfect feast,
To think I kill for her, at least,
Body and soul and peace and fame,
Alike youth's end and manhood's aim,
— So is my spirit, as flesh with sin,

Filled full, eaten out and in
With the face of her, the eyes of her,
The lips and little chin, the stir
Of shadow round her mouth; and she
— I 'll tell you — calmly would decree
That I should roast at a slow fire,
If that would compass her desire
And make her one whom they invite
To the famous ball to-morrow night.

There may be Heaven; there must be Hell;
Meantime, there is our Earth here, — well!

THE GLOVE.

"HEIGH-HO!" yawned one day King Francis,
     "Distance all value enhances!
When a man 's busy, why, leisure
Strikes him as wonderful pleasure.
'Faith, and at leisure once is he?
Straightway he wants to be busy.
Here we 've got peace; and aghast I 'm
Caught thinking war the true pastime!
Is there a reason in metre?
Give us your speech, master Peter!"
I who, if mortal dare say so,
Ne'er am at loss with my Naso,
"Sire," I replied, "joys prove cloudlets:
Men are the merest Ixions," —
Here the King whistled aloud, "Let 's
 . . . Heigh-ho . . . go look at our lions!"
Such are the sorrowful chances
If you talk fine to King Francis.

And so, to the court-yard proceeding,
Our company, Francis was leading,
Increased by new followers tenfold
Before he arrived at the penfold ;
Lords, ladies, like clouds which bedizen
At sunset the western horizon.
And Sir De Lorge pressed 'mid the foremost
With the dame he professed to adore most, —
O, what a face ! One by fits eyed
Her, and the horrible pitside ;
For the penfold surrounded a hollow
Which led where the eye scarce dared follow,
And shelved to the chamber secluded
Where Bluebeard, the great lion, brooded.
The King hailed his keeper, an Arab
As glossy and black as a searab,
And bade him make sport and at once stir
Up and out of his den the old monster.
They opened a hole in the wire-work
Across it, and dropped there a firework,
And fled ; one's heart's beating redoubled ;
A pause, while the pit's mouth was troubled,
The blackness and silence so utter,
By the firework's slow sparkling and sputter ;
Then earth in a sudden contortion
Gave out to our gaze her abortion !
Such a brute ! Were I friend Clement Marot
(Whose experience of nature 's but narrow,
And whose faculties move in no small mist
When he versifies David the Psalmist)
I should study that brute to describe you
Illum Juda Leonem de Tribu !
One's whole blood grew curdling and creepy
To see the black mane, vast and heapy,
The tail in the air stiff and straining,
The wide eyes, nor waxing nor waning,
As over the barrier which bounded
His platform, and us who surrounded
The barrier, they reached and they rested

On the space that might stand him in best stead :
For who knew, he thought, what the amazement,
The eruption of clatter and blaze meant,
And if, in this minute of wonder,
No outlet, 'mid lightning and thunder,
Lay broad, and, his shackles all shivered,
The lion at last was delivered ?
Ay, that was the open sky o'erhead !
And you saw by the flash on his forehead,
By the hope in those eyes wide and steady,
He was leagues in the desert already,
Driving the flocks up the mountain,
Or catlike couched hard by the fountain
To waylay the date-gathering negress :
So guarded he entrance or egress.
" How he stands ! " quoth the King : " we may well swear,
No novice, we 've won our spurs elsewhere,
And so can afford the confession,
We exercise wholesome discretion
In keeping aloof from his threshold ;
Once hold you, those jaws want no fresh hold,
Their first would too pleasantly purloin
The visitor's brisket or surloin :
But who 's he would prove so foolhardy ?
Not the best man of Marignan, pardie ! "

The sentence no sooner was uttered,
Than over the rails a glove fluttered,
Fell close to the lion, and rested :
The dame 't was, who flung it and jested
With life so, De Lorge had been wooing
For months past ; he sat there pursuing
His suit, weighing out with nonchalance
Fine speeches like gold from a balance.

Sound the trumpet, no true knight 's a tarrier !
De Lorge made one leap at the barrier,
Walked straight to the glove, — while the lion
Ne'er moved, kept his far-reaching eye on

The palm-tree-edged desert-spring's sapphire,
And the musky oiled skin of the Kaffir, —
Picked it up, and as calmly retreated,
Leaped back where the lady was seated,
And full in the face of its owner
Flung the glove, —

        " Your heart's queen, you dethrone her !
So should I," — cried the King, — " 't was mere vanity,
Not love, set that task to humanity ! "
Lords and ladies alike turned with loathing
From such a proved wolf in sheep's clothing.
Not so, I; for I caught an expression
In her brow's undisturbed self-possession
Amid the Court's scoffing and merriment, —
As if from no pleasing experiment
She rose, yet of pain not much heedful
So long as the process was needful, —
As if she had tried in a crucible,
To what "speeches like gold," were reducible,
And, finding the finest prove copper,
Felt the smoke in her face was but proper ;
To know what she had *not* to trust to,
Was worth all the ashes, and dust too.
She went out 'mid hooting and laughter ;
Clement Marot stayed ; I followed after,
And asked, as a grace, what it all meant, —
If she wished not the rash deed's recalment ?
" For I," — so I spoke, — " am a Poet :
Human nature, — behooves that I know it ! "

She told me, " Too long had I heard
Of the deed proved alone by the word :
For my love, — what De Lorge would not dare !
With my scorn, — what De Lorge could compare !
And the endless descriptions of death
He would brave when my lip formed a breath,
I must reckon as braved, or, of course,
Doubt his word, — and moreover, perforce,

For such gifts as no lady could spurn,
Must offer my love in return.
When I looked on your lion, it brought
All the dangers at once to my thought,
Encountered by all sorts of men,
Before he was lodged in his den, —
From the poor slave whose club or bare hands
Dug the trap, set the snare on the sands,
With no King and no Court to applaud,
By no shame, should he shrink, overawed,
Yet to capture the creature made shift,
That his rude boys might laugh at the gift,
To the page who last leaped o'er the fence
Of the pit, on no greater pretence
Than to get back the bonnet he dropped,
Lest his pay for a week should be stopped, —
So, wiser I judged it to make
One trial what 'death for my sake'
Really meant, while the power was yet mine,
Than to wait until time should define
Such a phrase not so simply as I,
Who took it to mean just 'to die.'
The blow a glove gives is but weak, —
Does the mark yet discolor my check ?
But when the heart suffers a blow,
Will the pain pass so soon, do you know?"

I looked, as away she was sweeping,
And saw a youth eagerly keeping
As close as he dared to the doorway:
No doubt that a noble should more weigh
His life than befits a plebeian;
And yet, had our brute been Nemean, —
(I judge by a certain calm fervor
The youth stepped with, forward to serve her)
— He'd have scarce thought you did him the worst turn
If you whispered "Friend, what you'd get, first earn!"
And when, shortly after, she carried
Her shame from the Court, and they married,

To that marriage some happiness, maugre
The voice of the Court, I dared augur.

For De Lorge, he made women with men vie,
Those in wonder and praise, these in envy;
And in short stood so plain a head taller
That he wooed and won . . . How do **you call her?**
The beauty, that rose in the sequel
To the King's love, who loved her a week well;
And 't was noticed he never would honor
De Lorge (who looked daggers upon her)
With the easy commission of stretching
His legs in the service, and fetching
His wife, from her chamber, those straying
Sad gloves she was always mislaying,
While the King took the closet to chat in, —
But of course this adventure came pat in;
And never the King told the story,
How bringing a glove brought **such** glory,
But the wife smiled, — " His nerves are grown firmer, —
Mine he brings now and utters no murmur ! "

"HOW THEY BROUGHT THE GOOD NEWS FROM GHENT TO AIX."

I SPRANG to the stirrup, and Joris, and he;
I galloped, Dirck galloped, we galloped all three;
" Good speed !" cried the watch, as the gate-bolts undrew;
" Speed !" echoed the wall to us galloping through;
Behind shut the postern, the lights sank **to rest,**
And into the midnight we galloped abreast.

Not a word to each other; we kept the great pace
Neck by neck, stride by stride, never changing our place;

I turned in my saddle and made its girths tight,
Then shortened each stirrup, and set the pique right,
Rebuckled the cheek-strap, chained slacker the bit,
Nor galloped less steadily Roland a whit.

'T was moonset at starting; but while we drew near
Lokeren, the cocks crew and twilight dawned clear;
At Boom, a great yellow star came out to see;
At Düffeld, 't was morning as plain as could be;
And from Mecheln church-steeple we heard the half-chime,
So Joris broke silence with, " Yet there is time !"

At Aerschot, up leaped of a sudden the sun,
And against him the cattle stood black every one,
To stare through the mist at us galloping past,
And I saw my stout galloper Roland at last,
With resolute shoulders, each butting away
The haze, as some bluff river headland its spray.

And his low head and crest, just one sharp ear bent back
For my voice, and the other pricked out on his track;
And one eye's black intelligence, — ever that glance
O'er its white edge at me, his own master, askance !
And the thick heavy spume-flakes which aye and anon
His fierce lips shook upwards in galloping on.

By Hasselt, Dirck groaned; and cried Joris, " Stay spur !
Your Roos galloped bravely, the fault 's not in her,
We 'll remember at Aix," — for one heard the quick wheeze
Of her chest, saw the stretched neck and staggering knees,
And sunk tail, and horrible heave of the flank,
As down on her haunches she shuddered and sank.

So we were left galloping, Joris and I,
Past Looz and past Tongres, no cloud in the sky;
The broad sun above laughed a pitiless laugh,
'Neath our feet broke the brittle bright stubble like chaff;
Till over by Dalhem a dome-spire sprang white,
And " Gallop," gasped Joris, " for Aix is in sight !"

"How they 'll greet us!"—and all in a moment his roan
Rolled neck and croup over, lay dead as a stone;
And there was my Roland to bear the whole weight
Of the news which alone could save Aix from her fate,
With his nostrils like pits full of blood to the brim,
And with circles of red for his eye-sockets' rim.

Then I cast loose my buff-coat, each holster let fall,
Shook off both my jack-boots, let go belt and all,

Stood up in the stirrup, leaned, patted his ear,
Called my Roland his pet-name, my horse without peer;
Clapped my hands, laughed and sang, any noise, bad or good,
Till at length into Aix Roland galloped and stood.

And all I remember is, friends flocking round
As I sat with his head 'twixt my knees on the ground,
And no voice but was praising this Roland of mine,
As I poured down his throat our last measure of wine,
Which (the burgesses voted by common consent)
Was no more than his due who brought good news from Ghent.

LOVE AMONG THE RUINS.

WHERE the quiet-colored end of evening smiles
            Miles and miles
On the solitary pastures where our sheep,
            Half-asleep,
Tinkle homeward through the twilight, stray or stop
            As they crop, —

Was the site once of a city great and gay,
            (So they say)
Of our country's very capital, its prince
            Ages since
Held his court in, gathered councils, wielding far
            Peace or war.

Now, — the country does not even boast a tree,
            As you see,
To distinguish slopes of verdure, certain rills
            From the hills
Intersect and give a name to, (else they run
            Into one)

Where the domed and daring palace shot **its spires**
      Up like fires
O'er the hundred-gated circuit of **a wall**
      Bounding all,
Made of marble, men might march on **nor be prest,**
      Twelve abreast.

And such plenty and perfection, see, of grass
      Never **was** !
Such a carpet as, this summer-time, o'erspreads
      And embeds
Every vestige of the city, guessed alone,
      Stock or stone —

Where a multitude of men breathed joy and woe
      Long ago ;
Lust of glory pricked their hearts **up, dread of shame**
      Struck them tame ;
And that glory and that shame alike, **the gold**
      Bought and sold.

Now, — the single little turret that remains
      On the plains,
By the caper overrooted, by the gourd
      Overscored,
While the patching houseleek's head of blossom winks
      Through the chinks —

Marks the basement whence a tower in ancient time
      Sprang sublime,
'**And** a burning ring all round, the chariots traced
      As they raced,
And the monarch and **his minions and his dames**
      Viewed the games.

And I know, while thus the quiet-colored **eve**
      Smiles to leave
To their folding, all our many-tinkling fleece
      In such peace,

And the slopes and rills in undistinguished gray
       Melt away —

That a girl with eager eyes and yellow hair
       Waits me there
In the turret, whence the charioteers caught soul
       For the goal,
When the king looked, where she looks now, breathless, dumb,
       Till I come.

But he looked upon the city, every side,
       Far and wide,
All the mountains topped with temples, all the glades'
       Colonnades,
All the causeys, bridges, aqueducts, — and then,
       All the men!

When I do come, she will speak not, she will stand,
       Either hand
On my shoulder, give her eyes the first embrace
       Of my face,
Ere we rush, ere we extinguish sight and speech
       Each on each.

In one year they sent a million fighters forth
       South and north,
And they built their gods a brazen pillar high
       As the sky,
Yet reserved a thousand chariots in full force, —
       Gold, of course.

O heart! O blood that freezes, blood that burns!
       Earth's returns
For whole centuries of folly, noise, and sin!
       Shut them in,
With their triumphs and their glories and the rest.
       Love is best!

A WOMAN'S LAST WORD.

LET 'S contend no more, Love,
    Strive nor weep, —
All be as before, Love,
   — Only sleep!

What so wild as words are?
   — I and thou
In debate, as birds are,
   Hawk on bough!

See the creature stalking
   While we speak, —
Hush and hide the talking,
   Cheek on cheek!

What so false as truth is,
   False to thee?
Where the serpent's tooth is,
   Shun the tree, —

Where the apple reddens
   Never pry, —
Lest we lose our Edens,
   Eve and I!

Be a god and hold me
   With a charm, —
Be a man and fold me
   With thine arm!

Teach me, only teach, Love!
   As I ought
I will speak thy speech, Love,
   Think thy thought, —

Meet, if thou require it,
  Both demands,
Laying flesh and spirit
  In thy hands!

That shall be to-morrow
  Not to-night:
I must bury sorrow
  Out of sight.

—Must a little weep, Love,
  —Foolish me!
And so fall asleep, Love,
  Loved by thee.

A SERENADE AT THE VILLA.

THAT was I, you heard last night
    When there rose no moon at all,
Nor, to pierce the strained and tight
    Tent of heaven, a planet small:
Life was dead, and so was light.

Not a twinkle from the fly,
    Not a glimmer from the worm.
When the crickets stopped their cry,
    When the owls forbore a term,
You heard music; that was I.

Earth turned in her sleep with pain,
    Sultrily suspired for proof:
In at heaven and out again,
    Lightning!—where it broke the roof,
Bloodlike, some few drops of rain.

What they could my words expressed,
  O my love, **my** all, my one!
Singing helped **the** verses best,
  And when singing's best was done,
To my lute I left the rest.

So wore night; the east was gray,
  White the broad-faced hemlock flowers;
Soon would come another day;
  Ere its first of heavy hours
Found me, I had past away.

What became of all the hopes,
  Words and song and lute as well?
Say, this struck you, — " When life gropes
  Feebly for the path where fell
Light last on the evening slopes,

" One **friend in that path shall be**
  To secure my steps from wrong;
One **to** count night day **for** me,
  Patient through the watches long,
Serving most with none to see."

Never say, — as something bodes, —
  " So the worst has yet a worse!
When life halts 'neath double loads,
  Better the task-master's curse
Than such music on the roads!

" When no moon **succeeds the sun,**
  Nor can pierce **the midnight's tent**
Any star, the smallest **one,**
  While some drops, **where** lightning **went,**
Show the final storm begun, —

" When **the** fire-fly hides **its** spot,
  When the garden-voices fail
In the darkness thick and hot, —

Shall another voice avail,
　That shape be where those are not?

" Has some plague a longer lease
　Proffering its help uncouth?
Can't one even die in peace?
　As one shuts one's eyes on youth,
Is that face the last one sees? "

O, how dark your villa was,
　Windows fast and obdurate!
How the garden grudged me grass
　Where I stood, — the iron gate
Ground its teeth to let me pass!

EVELYN HOPE.

BEAUTIFUL Evelyn Hope is dead!
　Sit and watch by her side an hour.
That is her book-shelf, this her bed;
　She plucked that piece of geranium-flower,
Beginning to die too, in the glass.
　Little has yet been changed, I think, —
The shutters are shut, no light may pass
　Save two long rays through the hinge's chink.

Sixteen years old when she died!
　Perhaps she had scarcely heard my name,
It was not her time to love: beside,
　Her life had many a hope and aim,
Duties enough and little cares,
　And now was quiet, now astir, —
Till God's hand beckoned unawares,
　And the sweet white brow is all of her.

Is it too late then, Evelyn Hope?
　What, your soul was pure and true,
The good stars met in your horoscope,
　Made you of spirit, fire, and dew, —
And just because I was thrice as old,
　And our paths in the world diverged so wide,
Each was naught to each, must I be told?
　We were fellow-mortals, naught beside?

No, indeed! for God above
　Is great to grant, as mighty to make,
And creates the love to reward the love, —
　I claim you still, for my own love's sake!
Delayed it may be for more lives yet,
　Through worlds I shall traverse, not a few, —
Much is to learn and much to forget
　Ere the time be come for taking you.

But the time will come, — at last it will,
　When, Evelyn Hope, what meant, I shall say,
In the lower earth, in the years long still,
　That body and soul so pure and gay?
Why your hair was amber, I shall divine,
　And your mouth of your own geranium's red, —
And what you would do with me, in fine,
　In the new life come in the old one's stead.

I have lived, I shall say, so much since then,
　Given up myself so many times,
Gained me the gains of various men,
　Ransacked the ages, spoiled the climes;

Yet one thing, one, in my soul's full scope,
　Either I missed or itself missed me, —
And I want and find you, Evelyn Hope!
　What is the issue? let us see!

I loved you, Evelyn, all the while;
　My heart seemed full as it could hold, —
There was place and to spare for the frank young smile,
　And the red young mouth, and the hair's young gold.
So, hush, — I will give you this leaf to keep, —
　See, I shut it inside the sweet cold hand.
There, that is our secret! go to sleep;
　You will wake, and remember, and understand.

MY STAR.

A LL that I know
　Of a certain star,
Is, it can throw
　(Like the angled spar)
Now a dart of red,
　Now a dart of blue,
Till my friends have said
　They would fain see, too,
My star that dartles the red and the blue!
Then it stops like a bird, — like a flower, hangs furled;
　They must solace themselves with the Saturn above it.
What matter to me if their star is a world?
　Mine has opened its soul to me; therefore I love it.

LOVE IN A LIFE.

ROOM after room,
   I hunt the house through
We inhabit together.
Heart, fear nothing, for, heart, thou shalt find her,
Next time, herself! — not the trouble behind her
Left in the curtain, the couch's perfume!
As she brushed it, the cornice-wreath blossomed anew,—
Yon looking-glass gleamed at the wave of her feather.

Yet the day wears,
And door succeeds door;
I try the fresh fortune, —
Range the wide house from the wing to the centre.
Still the same chance! she goes out as I enter.
Spend my whole day in the quest, — who cares?
But 't is twilight, you see, — with such suites to explore,
Such closets to search, such alcoves to importune!

LIFE IN A LOVE.

ESCAPE me?
   Never,
      Beloved!
While I am I, and you are you,
   So long as the world contains us both,
   Me the loving and you the loth,
While the one eludes, must the other pursue.
My life is a fault at last, I fear, —
   It seems too much like a fate, indeed!

Though I do my best I shall scarce succeed, —
But what if I fail of my purpose here?
It is but to keep the nerves at strain,
  To dry one's eyes and laugh at a fall,
And baffled, get up to begin again, —
  So the chace takes up one's life, that 's all.
While, look but once from your furthest bound,
  At me so deep in the dust and dark,
No sooner the old hope drops to ground
  Than a new one, straight to the selfsame mark,
        I shape me, —
        Ever
        Removed!

MEMORABILIA.

A H, did you once see Shelley plain,
      And did he stop and speak to you?
And did you speak to him again?
  How strange it seems, and new!

But you were living before that,
  And you are living after,
And the memory I started at, —
  My starting moves your laughter!

I crossed a moor with a name of its own
  And a use in the world no doubt,
Yet a hand's-breadth of it shines alone
  'Mid the blank miles round about, —

For there I picked up on the heather
  And there I put inside my breast
A moulted feather, an eagle-feather, —
  Well, I forget the rest.

AFTER.

TAKE the cloak from his face, and at first
Let the corpse do its worst.

How he lies in his rights of a man!
Death has done all death can.
And, absorbed in the new life he leads,
He recks not, he heeds
Nor his wrong nor my vengeance, — both strike
On his senses alike,
And are lost in the solemn and strange
Surprise of the change.
Ha, what avails death to erase
His offence, my disgrace?
I would we were boys as of old
In the field, by the fold, —
His outrage, God's patience, man's scorn
Were so easily borne.

I stand here now, he lies in his place, —
Cover the face.

IN THREE DAYS.

SO, I shall see her in three days
And just one night, but nights are short,
Then two long hours, and that is morn.
See how I come, unchanged, unworn, —
Feel, where my life broke off from thine,
How fresh the splinters keep and fine, —
Only a touch and we combine!

Too long, this time of year, the days!
But nights — at least the nights are short.
As night shows where her one moon is,
A hand's-breadth of pure light and bliss,
So, life's night gives my lady birth
And my eyes hold her! what is worth
The rest of heaven, the rest of earth?

O loaded curls, release your store
Of warmth and scent as once before
The tingling hair did, lights and darks
Out-breaking into fairy sparks
When under curl and curl I pried
After the warmth and scent inside
Through lights and darks how manifold, —
The dark inspired, the light controlled!
As early Art embrowned the gold.

What great fear — should one say, "Three days
That change the world, might change as well
Your fortune; and if joy delays,
Be happy that no worse befell."
What small fear — if another says,
"Three days and one short night beside
May throw no shadow on your ways;
But years must teem with change untried,
With chance not easily defied,
With an end somewhere undescried."
No fear! — or if a fear be born
This minute, it dies out in scorn.
Fear? I shall see her in three days
And one night, now the nights are short,
Then just two hours, and that is morn.

IN A YEAR.

NEVER any more
    While I live,
Need I hope to see his face
    As before.
Once his love grown chill,
    Mine may strive, —
Bitterly we re-embrace,
    Single still.

Was it something said,
    Something done,
Vexed him ? was it touch of hand,
    Turn of head ?
Strange ! that very way
    Love begun.
I as little understand
    Love's decay.

When I sewed or drew,
  I recall
How he looked as if I sang,
  — Sweetly too.
If I spoke a word,
  First of all
Up his cheek the color sprang,
  Then he heard.

Sitting by my side,
  At my feet,
So he breathed the air I breathed,
  Satisfied!
I, too, at love's brim
  Touched the sweet:
I would die if death bequeathed
  Sweet to him.

"Speak, I love thee best!"
  He exclaimed.
"Let thy love my own foretell," —
  I confessed:
"Clasp my heart on thine
  Now unblamed,
Since upon thy soul as well
  Hangeth mine!"

Was it wrong to own,
  Being truth?
Why should all the giving prove
  His alone?
I had wealth and ease,
  Beauty, youth, —
Since my lover gave me love,
  I gave these.

That was all I meant,
  — To be just,
And the passion I had raised
  To content.

Since he chose to change
  Gold for dust,
If I gave him what he praised
  Was it strange?

Would he loved me yet,
  On and on,
While I found some way undreamed
  — Paid my debt!
Gave more life and more,
  Till, all gone,
He should smile, " She never seemed
  Mine before.

" What, — she felt the while,
  Must I think?
Love 's so different with us men,"
  He should smile.
" Dying for my sake, —
  White and pink!
Can't we touch these bubbles then
  But they break? "

Dear, the pang is brief.
  Do thy part,
Have thy pleasure.   How perplext
  Grows belief!
Well, this cold clay clod
  Was man's heart.
Crumble it, — and what comes next?
  Is it God?

"DE GUSTIBUS —"

YOUR ghost will walk, you lover of trees,
     (If loves remain)
    In an English lane,
By a cornfield-side a-flutter with poppies.
Hark, those two in the hazel coppice, —
A boy and a girl, if the good fates please,
     Making love, say, —
     The happier they!
Draw yourself up from the light of the moon,
And let them pass, as they will too soon,
     With the bean-flowers' boon,
     And the blackbird's tune,
     And May, and June!

What I love best in all the world,
Is, a castle, precipice-encurled,
In a gash of the wind-grieved Apennine.
Or look for me, old fellow of mine
(If I get my head from out the mouth
O' the grave, and loose my spirit's bands,
And come again to the land of lands), —
In a seaside house to the farther south,
Where the baked cicalas die of drouth,
And one sharp tree ('t is a cypress) stands,
By the many hundred years red-rusted,
Rough iron-spiked, ripe fruit-o'ercrusted,
My sentinel to guard the sands
To the water's edge. For, what expands
Without the house, but the great opaque
Blue breadth of sea, and not a break?
While, in the house, forever crumbles
Some fragment of the frescoed walls,
From blisters where a scorpion sprawls.
A girl barefooted brings and tumbles

Down on the pavement, green-flesh melons,
And says there 's news to-day, — the king
Was shot at, touched in the liver-wing,
Goes with his Bourbon arm in a sling.
— She hopes they have not caught the felons.
    Italy, my Italy!
Queen Mary's saying serves for me, —
    (When fortune's malice
    Lost her, Calais.)
Open my heart and you will see
Graved inside of it, "Italy."
Such lovers old are I and she;
So it always was, so it still shall be!

WOMEN AND ROSES.

I DREAM of a red-rose tree.
  And which of its roses three
Is the dearest rose to me?

Round and round, like a dance of snow
In a dazzling drift, as its guardians, go
Floating the women faded for ages,
Sculptured in stone, on the poet's pages.
Then follow the women fresh and gay,
Living and loving and loved to-day.
Last, in the rear, flee the multitude of maidens,
Beauties unborn. And all, to one cadence,
They circle their rose on my rose-tree.

    Dear rose, thy term is reached,
    Thy leaf hangs loose and bleached:
    Bees pass it unimpeached.
    6

Stay then, stoop, since I cannot climb,
You, great shapes of the antique time !
How shall I fix you, fire you, freeze you,
Break my heart at your feet to please you ?
O to possess, and be possessed !
Hearts that beat 'neath each pallid breast !
But once of love, the poesy, the passion,
Drink once and die ! — In vain, the same fashion,
They circle their rose on my rose-tree.

Dear rose, thy joy 's undimmed ;
Thy cup is ruby-rimmed,
Thy cup's heart nectar-brimmed.

Deep as drops from a statue's plinth
The bee sucked in by the hyacinth,
So will I bury me while burning,
Quench like him at a plunge my yearning,
Eyes in your eyes, lips on your lips !
Fold me fast where the cincture slips,
Prison all my soul in eternities of pleasure !
Girdle me once ! But no, — in their old measure
They circle their rose on my rose-tree.

Dear rose without a thorn,
Thy bud 's the babe unborn,
First streak of a new morn.

Wings, lend wings for the cold, the clear !
What 's far conquers what is near.
Roses will bloom nor want beholders,
Sprung from the dust where our own flesh moulders.
What shall arrive with the cycle's change ?
A novel grace and a beauty strange.
I will make an Eve, be the artist that began her,
Shaped her to his mind ! — Alas ! in like manner
They circle their rose on my rose-tree.

THE GUARDIAN-ANGEL:

A PICTURE AT FANO.

DEAR and great Angel, wouldst thou only leave
    That child, when thou **hast** done with him, for **me**!
Let me sit all the day **here, that when eve**
    Shall find performed thy special ministry
And time come for departure, thou, suspending
Thy flight, may'st see another child for tending,
    Another still, to quiet and retrieve.

Then I shall feel thee step one step, **no more,**
    From where thou standest now, to **where I gaze,**
And suddenly my head be covered o'er
    With those wings, white above the **child** who prays
Now on that tomb, — **and** I shall feel thee guarding
Me, out **of all the world; for me,** discarding
    Yon heaven thy home, that waits and opes its door!

I would not look up thither past **thy** head
    Because the **door** opes, like that child, I know,
For I should **have** thy gracious face instead,
    Thou bird of God! And wilt thou bend me **low**
Like him, and lay, like his, my hands together,
And lift them up to pray, **and** gently tether
    Me, **as** thy lamb there, with thy garment's **spread?**

If this was ever **granted, I** would rest
    My head beneath **thine,** while thy healing hands
Close-covered both my eyes beside thy breast,
    Pressing the brain, which too much thought expands,
Back to its proper size again, and smoothing
Distortion down till every nerve had soothing,
    And all lay quiet, happy, and supprest.

How soon all worldly wrong would be repaired!
    I think how I should view the earth and skies
And sea, when once again my brow was bared
    After thy healing, with such different eyes.
O world, as God has made it! all is beauty:
And knowing this, is love, and love is duty.
    What further may be sought for or declared?

Guercino drew this angel I saw teach
    (Alfred, dear friend,) — that little child to pray,
Holding the little hands up, each to each
    Pressed gently, — with his own head turned away
Over the earth where so much lay before him
Of work to do, though heaven was opening o'er him,
    And he was left at Fano by the beach.

We were at Fano, and three times we went
    To sit and see him in his chapel there,
And drink his beauty to our soul's content,
    — My angel with me too: and since I care
For dear Guercino's fame, (to which in power
And glory comes this picture for a dower,
    Fraught with a pathos so magnificent,)

And since he did not work so earnestly
    At all times, and has else endured some wrong, —
I took one thought his picture struck from me,
    And spread it out, translating it to song.
My Love is here.   Where are you, dear old friend?
How rolls the Wairoa at your world's far end?
    This is Ancona, yonder is the sea.

TWO IN THE CAMPAGNA.

I WONDER do you feel to-day
  As I have felt, since, hand in hand,
We sat down on the grass, to stray
  In spirit better through the land,
This morn of Rome and May ?

For me, I touched a thought, I know,
  Has tantalized me many times,
(Like turns of thread the spiders throw
  Mocking across our path) for rhymes
To catch at and let go.

Help me to hold it : first it left
  The yellowing fennel, run to seed
There, branching from the brickwork's cleft,
  Some old tomb's ruin : yonder weed
Took up the floating weft,

Where one small orange cup amassed
  Five beetles, — blind and green they grope
Among the honey-meal, — and last
  Everywhere on the grassy slope
I traced it. Hold it fast !

The champaign with its endless fleece
  Of feathery grasses everywhere !
Silence and passion, joy and peace,
  An everlasting wash of air, —
Rome's ghost since her decease.

Such life there, through such lengths of hours,
  Such miracles performed in play,
Such primal naked forms of flowers,
  Such letting Nature have her way
While Heaven looks from its towers.

How say you?   Let us, O my dove,
   Let us be unashamed of soul,
As earth lies bare to heaven above.
   How is it under our control
To love or not to love?

I would that you were all to me,
   You that are just so much, no more,—
Nor yours, nor mine,—nor slave, nor free!
   Where does the fault lie? what the core
Of the wound, since wound must be?

I would I could adopt your will,
   See with your eyes, and set my heart
Beating by yours, and drink my fill
   At your soul's springs,— your part, my part
In life, for good and ill.

No.   I yearn upward,— touch you close,
   Then stand away.   I kiss your cheek,
Catch your soul's warmth,— I pluck the rose
   And love it more than tongue can speak,—
Then the good minute goes.

Already how am I so far
   Out of that minute?   Must I go
Still like the thistle-ball, no bar,
   Onward, whenever light winds blow,
Fixed by no friendly star?

Just when I seemed about to learn!
   Where is the thread now?   Off again!
The old trick!   Only I discern —
   Infinite passion and the pain
Of finite hearts that yearn.

THE PATRIOT.

AN OLD STORY.

IT was roses, roses, all the way,
  With myrtle mixed in my **path** like mad.
The house-roofs seemed to heave and sway,
  The church-spires flamed, such flags they **had**,
A year ago on this very day!

The air broke into a mist with bells,
  The old walls rocked with the crowds and cries.
Had I said, " Good folks, mere noise repels, —
  But give me your sun from yonder skies ! "
They had answered, " And afterward, **what else ?** "

Alack, it was **I** who **leaped at the sun**,
  To give it my **loving friends** to **keep.**
Naught man could do, **have I** left **undone**,
  And **you** see my harvest, what I reap
This **very** day, now a year is run.

There 's nobody on the house-tops now, —
  Just a palsied few at the windows set, —
For the best of the sight is, all allow,
  At the Shambles' Gate, — or, better **yet**,
By the very scaffold's foot, **I trow.**

I go in the rain, and, more than **needs**,
  A rope cuts both **my** wrists behind,
And I think, by the **feel**, my forehead bleeds,
  For they fling, whoever has a mind,
Stones at me for my **year's misdeeds.**

Thus I entered Brescia, and thus I go!
  In such triumphs, people have dropped down dead.
"Thou, paid by the World, — what dost thou owe
  Me?" God might have questioned: but now instead
'T is God shall requite! I am safer so.

A GRAMMARIAN'S FUNERAL.

[*Time.* — Shortly after the revival of learning in Europe.]

LET us begin, and carry up this corpse,
    Singing together.
Leave we the common crofts, the vulgar thorpes,
    Each in its tether
Sleeping safe on the bosom of the plain,
    Cared-for till cock-crow.
Look out if yonder 's not the day again
    Rimming the rock-row !
That 's the appropriate country, — there, man's thought,
    Rarer, intenser,
Self-gathered for an outbreak, as it ought,
    Chafes in the censer !
Leave we the unlettered plain its herd and crop :
    Seek we sepulture
On a tall mountain, citied to the top,
    Crowded with culture !
All the peaks soar, but one the rest excels ;
    Clouds overcome it ;
No, yonder sparkle is the citadel's
    Circling its summit !   •
Thither our path lies, — wind we up the heights, —
    Wait ye the warning ?
Our low life was the level's and the night's ;
    He 's for the morning !
Step to a tune, square chests, erect the head,
    'Ware the beholders !
This is our master, famous, calm, and dead,
    Borne on our shoulders.

Sleep, crop and herd !   Sleep, darkling thorpe and croft,
    Safe from the weather !
He, whom we convoy to his grave aloft,
    Singing together,

He was a man born with thy face and throat,
    Lyric Apollo!
Long he lived nameless: how should spring take note
    Winter would follow?
Till lo, the little touch, and youth was gone!
    Cramped and diminished,
Moaned he, "New measures, other feet anon!
    My dance is finished?"
No, that's the world's way! (keep the mountain-side,
    Make for the city.)
He knew the signal, and stepped on **with pride**
    Over men's pity;
Left play for work, and grappled **with the world**
    Bent on escaping:
"What's in **the scroll**," quoth he, "thou keepest furled?
    Show me their shaping,
Theirs, who most studied man, the bard and sage, —
    Give!" — So he gowned him,
Straight got by **heart that book to its last page:**
    Learned, we found him!
Yea, but we found him bald, too, — eyes like lead,
    Accents uncertain:
"**Time to taste** life," another would have said,
    "**Up** with the curtain!"
This man said rather, "Actual life comes next?
    Patience a moment!
Grant I have mastered learning's crabbed text,
    Still, there's the comment.
Let me know all. Prate not of most or least,
    Painful or **easy**:
Even to the crumbs I'd fain eat up the feast,
    Ay, nor feel queasy!"
O, such a life as he resolved **to live,**
    When he had learned it,
When he had gathered all books had **to give;**
    Sooner, he spurned it!
Image the whole, then execute the parts, —
    Fancy the fabric
Quite, ere **you** build, ere steel strike fire from quartz,
    Ere mortar dab brick!

(Here 's the town-gate reached : there 's the market-place
    Gaping before us.)
Yea, this in him was the peculiar grace
    (Hearten our chorus)
Still before living he 'd learn how to live, —
    No end to learning.
Earn the means first, — God surely will contrive
    Use for our earning.
Others mistrust and say, — " But time escapes, —
    Live now or never ! "
He said, " What 's Time ? leave Now for dogs and apes !
    Man has Forever."
Back to his book then : deeper drooped his head ;
    Calculus racked him :
Leaden before, his eyes grew dross of lead ;
    Tussis attacked him,
" Now, Master, take a little rest ! " — not he !
    (Caution redoubled !
Step two a-breast, the way winds narrowly.)
    Not a whit troubled,
Back to his studies, fresher than at first,
    Fierce as a dragon
He (soul-hydroptic with a sacred thirst)
    Sucked at the flagon.
O, if we draw a circle premature,
    Heedless of far gain,
Greedy for quick returns of profit, sure,
    Bad is our bargain !
Was it not great ? did he not throw on God,
    (He loves the burthen) —
God's task to make the heavenly period
    Perfect the earthen ?
Did not he magnify the mind, show clear
    Just what it all meant ?
He would not discount life, as fools do here,
    Paid by instalment !
He ventured neck or nothing, — heaven's success
    Found, or earth's failure :
" Wilt thou trust death or not ? " he answered, " Yes.
    Hence with life's pale lure ! "

That low man seeks a little thing to do,
    Sees it and does it:
This high man, with a great thing to pursue,
    Dies ere he knows it.
That low man goes on adding one to one,
    His hundred's soon hit:
This high man, aiming at a million,
    Misses an unit.
That, has the world here, — should he need the next,
    Let the world mind him!
This, throws himself on God, and unperplext
    Seeking shall find Him.
So, with the throttling hands of Death at strife,
    Ground he at grammar;
Still, through the rattle, parts of speech were rife.
    While he could stammer
He settled *Hoti's* business, — let it be! —
    Properly based *Oun*, —
Gave us the doctrine of the enclitic *De*,
    Dead from the waist down.
Well, here's the platform, here's the proper place.
    Hail to your purlieus
All ye highfliers of the feathered race,
    Swallows and curlews!
Here's the top-peak! the multitude below
    Live, for they can there.
This man decided not to Live but Know, —
    Bury this man there?
Here, — here's his place, where meteors shoot, clouds form,
    Lightnings are loosened,
Stars come and go! let joy break with the storm, —
    Peace let the dew send!
Lofty designs must close in like effects:
    Loftily lying,
Leave him, — still loftier than the world suspects,
    Living and dying.

THE CONFESSIONAL.

[SPAIN.]

IT is a lie, — their Priests, their Pope,
  Their Saints, their . . . all they fear or hope
Are lies, and lies, — there! through my door
And ceiling, there! and walls and floor,
There, lies, they lie, shall still be hurled,
Till spite of them I reach the world!

You think Priests just and holy men!
Before they put me in this den,
I was a human creature too,
With flesh and blood like one of you,
A girl that laughed in beauty's pride
Like lilies in your world outside.

I had a lover, — shame avaunt!
This poor wrenched body, grim and gaunt,
Was kissed all over till it burned,
By lips the truest, love e'er turned
His heart's own tint: one night they kissed
My soul out in a burning mist.

So, next day when the accustomed train
Of things grew round my sense again,
" That is a sin," I said, — and slow
With downcast eyes to church I go,
And pass to the confession-chair,
And tell the old mild father there.

But when I falter Beltran's name,
" Ha ?" quoth the father; " much I blame
The sin; yet wherefore idly grieve ?
Despair not, — strenuously retrieve !
Nay, I will turn this love of thine
To lawful love, almost divine.

" For he is young, and led astray,
This Beltran, and he schemes, men say,
To change the laws of church and state ;
So, thine shall be an angel's fate,
Who, ere the thunder breaks, should roll
Its cloud away and save his soul.

" For, when he lies upon thy breast,
Thou mayst demand and be possessed
Of all his plans, and next day steal
To me, and all those plans reveal,

That I and every priest, to purge
His soul, may fast and use the scourge."

That father's beard was long and white,
With love and truth his brow seemed bright;
I went back, all on fire with joy,
And, that same evening, bade the boy,
Tell me, as lovers should, heart-free,
Something to prove his love of me.

He told me what he would not tell
For hope of Heaven or fear of Hell;
And I lay listening in such pride,
And, soon as he had left my side,
Tripped to the church by morning-light
To save his soul in his despite.

I told the father all his schemes,
Who were his comrades, what their dreams,
"And now make haste," I said, "to pray
The one spot from his soul away:
To-night he comes, but not the same
Will look!" At night he never came.

Nor next night: on the after-morn,
I went forth with a strength new-born:
The church was empty; something drew
My steps into the street; I knew
It led me to the market-place, —
Where, lo! — on high — the father's face!

That horrible black scaffold drest, —
The stapled block . . . God sink the rest!
That head strapped back, that blinding vest,
Those knotted hands and naked breast, —
Till near one busy hangman pressed, —
And — on the neck these arms caressed. . . .

No part in aught they hope or fear!
No Heaven with them, no Hell, — and here,

No Earth, not **so much** space **as pens**
My body in their worst of **dens**
But shall bear God and Man my cry, —
Lies, — lies, again, — and still, they lie!

ONE WAY OF LOVE.

ALL June I bound the rose in sheaves.
Now, rose by rose, I strip the leaves,
And strew them where Pauline may pass.
She will not turn **aside?** Alas!
Let them lie. Suppose **they die?**
The chance **was they might take her eye.**

How many **a** month **I** strove to suit
These stubborn fingers to the lute!
To-day I venture all I know.
She will not hear my music? **So!**
Break the string, fold music's wing.
Suppose Pauline had bade me sing!

My whole life long **I learned to love.**
This hour my utmost art I prove
And speak **my** passion. — Heaven or hell?
She will not give me heaven? 'T is well!
Lose who may, I still can say,
Those who win heaven, blest are they.

ANOTHER WAY OF LOVE.

JUNE was not over,
　　Though past the full,
And the best of her roses
　　Had **yet to** blow,
　　When **a man I** know
(But shall **not discover,**
　　Since ears are dull,
　　And time discloses)
Turned **him and said,** with a man's true air,
Half sighing a smile in a yawn, as 't were, —
" If I tire of your June, will she greatly care ? "

　　Well, Dear, in-doors with you !
　　　True, serene deadness
　　Tries a man's temper.
　　　What 's in the blossom
　　June wears on her bosom ?
　　Can it clear scores with you ?
　　　Sweetness and redness,
　　　Eadem semper !
Go, let me care for it greatly or slightly !
If June mends her bowers now, your hand left unsightly
By plucking their roses, — **my** June will do rightly.

　　And after, **for** pastime,
　　　If June **be** refulgent
　　With flowers in completeness,
　　　All petals, no prickles,
　　　Delicious as trickles
　　Of wine poured **at** mass-time, —
　　　And choose One indulgent
　　　To redness and sweetness :
Or if, with experience of man and of spider,
She use my June-lightning, the strong insect-ridder,
To stop the fresh spinning, — why, June will consider.
　7

MISCONCEPTIONS.

THIS is a spray the Bird clung to,
  Making it blossom with pleasure,
Ere the high tree-top she sprung to,
  Fit for her nest and her treasure.
  O, what a hope beyond measure
Was the poor spray's, which the flying feet hung to,—
  So to be singled out, built in, and sung to!

This is a heart the Queen leant on,
  Thrilled in a minute erratic,
Ere the true bosom she bent on,
  Meet for love's regal dalmatic.
  O, what a fancy ecstatic
Was the poor heart's, ere the wanderer went on,—
  Love to be saved for it, proffered to, spent on!

ONE WORD MORE.

TO E. B. B.

THERE they are, my fifty men and women
  Naming me the fifty poems finished!
Take them, Love, the book and me together.
Where the heart lies, let the brain lie also.

Rafael made a century of sonnets,
Made and wrote them in a certain volume
Dinted with the silver-pointed pencil
Else he only used to draw Madonnas:

These, the world **might** view, — but One, **the volume.**
Who that **one,** you **ask?** Your **heart instructs you.**
Did she live and love **it all** her lifetime?
Did she drop, his lady of the sonnets,
Die, and let it drop beside her pillow
Where it lay in place of Rafael's glory,
Rafael's cheek so duteous and so loving, —
Cheek, **the** world **was** wont to hail a painter's,
Rafael's **cheek,** her **love** had turned a poet's?

You and I would rather read that volume,
(Taken to his beating bosom by it,)
Lean and list the bosom-beats of Rafael,
Would we not? than wonder at Madonnas, —
Her, **San Sisto names,** and Her, Foligno,
Her, **that** visits Florence in a vision,
Her, **that** 's left with lilies in the Louvre, —
Seen by us and **all the** world in circle.

You and I will never **read** that volume.
Guido Reni, like his own eye's **apple**
Guarded long the treasure-book **and loved it.**
Guido Reni dying, all Bologna
Cried, and the world with it, " Ours — the treasure! "
Suddenly, as rare things will, it vanished.

Dante once prepared to paint an angel :
Whom to please? You whisper " Beatrice."
While he mused and traced it and retraced it,
(Peradventure with a pen corroded
Still by drops of that hot ink he dipped for,
When, his left-hand i' the hair o' the **wicked,**
Back he held the brow and pricked its stigma,
Bit into the live man's flesh for parchment,
Loosed him, laughed to see **the** writing rankle,
Let the wretch go festering through Florence,) —
Dante, who loved **well because** he hated,
Hated wickedness that hinders loving,
Dante standing, studying his angel, —

In there broke the folk of his Inferno.
Says he, — " Certain people of importance "
(Such he gave his daily, dreadful line to)
Entered and would seize, forsooth, the poet.
Says the poet, — " Then I stopped my painting."

You and I would rather see that angel,
Painted by the tenderness of Dante,
Would we not ? — than read a fresh Inferno.

You and I will never see that picture.
, While he mused on love and Beatrice,
While he softened o'er his outlined angel,
In they broke, those "people of importance":
We and Bice bear the loss forever.

What of Rafael's sonnets, Dante's picture ?

This : no artist lives and loves that longs not
Once, and only once, and for One only,
(Ah, the prize !) to find his love a language
Fit and fair and simple and sufficient, —
Using nature that 's an art to others,
Not, this one time, art that 's turned his nature.
Ay, of all the artists living, loving,
None but would forego his proper dowry, —
Does he paint ? he fain would write a poem, —
Does he write ? he fain would paint a picture,
Put to proof art alien to the artist's,
Once, and only once, and for One only,
So to be the man and leave the artist,
Save the man's joy, miss the artist's sorrow.

Wherefore ?　Heaven's gift takes earth's abatement !
He who smites the rock and spreads the water,
Bidding drink and live a crowd beneath him,
Even he, the minute makes immortal,
Proves, perchance, his mortal in the minute,
Desecrates, belike, the deed in doing.

While he smites, how can he but remember,
So he smote before, in such a peril,
When they stood and mocked, — "Shall smiting help us?"
When they drank and sneered, — "A stroke is easy!"
When they wiped their mouths and went their journey,
Throwing him for thanks, — "But drought was pleasant."
Thus old memories mar the actual triumph;
Thus the doing savors of disrelish;
Thus achievement lacks a gracious somewhat;
O'er-importuned brows becloud the mandate,
Carelessness or consciousness, the gesture.
For he bears an ancient wrong about him,
Sees and knows again those phalanxed faces,
Hears, yet one time more, the 'customed prelude, —
"How shouldst thou, of all men, smite, and save us?"
Guesses what is like to prove the sequel, —
"Egypt's flesh-pots, — nay, the drought was better."

O, the crowd must have emphatic warrant!
Theirs, the Sinai-forehead's cloven brilliance,
Right-arm's rod-sweep, tongue's imperial fiat.
Never dares the man put off the prophet.

Did he love one face from out the thousands,
(Where she Jethro's daughter, white and wifely,
Were she but the Æthiopian bond-slave,)
He would envy yon dumb patient camel,
Keeping a reserve of scanty water
Meant to save his own life in the desert;
Ready in the desert to deliver
(Kneeling down to let his breast be opened)
Hoard and life together for his mistress.

I shall never, in the years remaining,
Paint you pictures, no, nor carve you statues,
Make you music that should all-express me;
So it seems: I stand on my attainment.
This of verse alone, one life allows me;
Verse and nothing else have I to give you.

Other heights in other lives, God willing, —
All the gifts from all the heights, your own, Love!

Yet a semblance of resource avails us, —
Shade so finely touched, love's sense must seize it.
Take these lines, look lovingly and nearly,
Lines I write the first time and the last time.
He who works in fresco, steals a hair-brush,
Curbs the liberal hand, subservient proudly,
Cramps his spirit, crowds its all in little,
Makes a strange art of an art familiar,
Fills his lady's missal-marge with flowerets.
He who blows through bronze, may breathe through silver,
Fitly serenade a slumbrous princess.
He who writes, may write for once, as I do.

Love, you saw me gather men and women,
Live or dead or fashioned by my fancy,
Enter each and all, and use their service,
Speak from every mouth, — the speech, a poem.
Hardly shall I tell my joys and sorrows,
Hopes and fears, belief and disbelieving:
I am mine and yours, — the rest be all men's,
Karshook, Cleon, Norbert, and the fifty.
Let me speak this once in my true person,
Not as Lippo, Roland, or Andrea,
Though the fruit of speech be just this sentence, —
Pray you, look on these my men and women,
Take and keep my fifty poems finished;
Where my heart lies, let my brain lie also!
Poor the speech; be how I speak, for all things.

Not but that you know me! Lo! the moon's self!
Here in London, yonder late in Florence,
Still we find her face, the thrice-transfigured.
Curving on a sky imbrued with color,
Drifted over Fiesole by twilight,
Came she, our new crescent of a hair's-breadth.
Full she flared it, lamping Samminiato,

Rounder 'twixt the cypresses and rounder,
Perfect till the nightingales applauded.
Now, a piece of her old self, impoverished,
Hard to greet, she traverses the house-roofs,
Hurries with unhandsome thrift of silver,
Goes dispiritedly, — glad to finish.

What, there 's nothing in the moon note-worthy ?
Nay, — for if that moon could love a mortal,
Use, to charm him (so to fit a fancy)
All her magic ('t is the old sweet mythos)
She would turn a new side to her mortal,
Side unseen of herdsman, huntsman, steersman, —
Blank to Zoroaster on his terrace,
Blind to Galileo on his turret,
Dumb to Homer, dumb to Keats, — him, even !
Think, the wonder of the moonstruck mortal, —
When she turns round, comes again in heaven,
Opens out anew for worse or better ?
Proves she like some portent of an iceberg
Swimming full upon the ship it founders,
Hungry with huge teeth of splintered crystals ?
Proves she as the paved-work of a sapphire
Seen by Moses when he climbed the mountain ?
Moses, Aaron, Nadab and Abihu
Climbed and saw the very God, the Highest,
Stand upon the paved-work of a sapphire.
Like the bodied heaven in his clearness
Shone the stone, the sapphire of that paved-work,
When they ate and drank and saw God also !

What were seen ?   None knows, none ever shall know.
Only this is sure, — the sight were other,
Not the moon's same side, born late in Florence,
Dying now impoverished here in London.
God be thanked, the meanest of his creatures
Boasts two soul-sides, one to face the world with,
One to show a woman when he loves her.

This I say of me, but think of you, Love!
This to you, — yourself my moon of poets!
Ah, but that's the world's side, — there's the wonder, —
Thus they see you, praise you, think they know you.
There, in turn I stand with them and praise you,
Out of my own self, I dare to phrase it.
But the best is when I glide from out them,
Cross a step or two of dubious twilight,
Come out on the other side, the novel
Silent silver lights and darks undreamed of,
Where I hush and bless myself with silence.

O, their Rafael of the dear Madonnas,
O, their Dante of the dread Inferno,
Wrote one song — and in my brain I sing it,
Drew one angel — borne, see, on my bosom!

MEETING AT NIGHT.

THE gray sea and the long black land;
   And the yellow half-moon large and low;
And the startled little waves that leap
In fiery ringlets from their sleep,
As I gain the cove with pushing prow,
And quench its speed in the slushy sand.

Then a mile of warm sea-scented beach;
Three fields to cross till a farm appears;
A tap at the pane, the quick sharp scratch
And blue spurt of a lighted match,
And a voice less loud, through its joys and fears,
Than the two hearts beating each to each!

PARTING AT MORNING.

ROUND the cape of a sudden came the sea,
      And the sun looked over the mountain's rim, —
And straight was a path of gold for him,
And the need of a world of men for me.

PROSPICE.

FEAR death? — to feel the fog in my throat,
      The mist in my face,
When the snows begin, and the blasts denote
      I am nearing the place,
The power of the night, the press of the storm,
      The post of the foe;
Where he stands, the Arch Fear in a visible form,
      Yet the strong man must go:
For the journey is done and the summit attained,
      And the barriers fall,
Though a battle 's to fight ere the guerdon be gained,
      The reward of it all.
I was ever a fighter, so, — one fight more,
      The best and the last!
I would hate that death bandaged my eyes, and forbore,
      And bade me creep past.
No! let me taste the whole of it, fare like my peers
      The heroes of old,
Bear the brunt, in a minute pay glad life's arrears
      Of pain, darkness, and cold.
For sudden the worst turns the best to the brave,
      The black minute 's at end,

And the elements' rage, the fiend-voices that rave,
    Shall dwindle, shall blend,
Shall change, shall become first a peace, then a joy,
    Then a light, then thy breast,
O thou soul of my soul! I shall clasp thee again,
    And with God be the rest!

MAY AND DEATH.

I WISH that when you died last May,
  Charles, there had died along with you
Three parts of spring's delightful things;
    Ay, and, for me, the fourth part too.

A foolish thought, and worse, perhaps!
  There must be many a pair of friends
Who, arm in arm, deserve the warm
    Moon-births and the long evening-ends.

So, for their sakes, be May still May!
  Let their new time, as mine of old,
Do all it did for me: I bid
    Sweet sights and sounds throng manifold.

Only, one little sight, one plant,
  Woods have in May, that starts up green
Save a sole streak which, so to speak,
    Is spring's blood, spilt its leaves between, —

That, they might spare; a certain wood
  Might miss the plant; their loss were small:
But I, — whene'er the leaf grows there,
    Its drop comes from my heart, that's all.

THE DOORWAY.

The swe   as set her six young on the rail,
       A   s seaward :
The water 's   ipes like a snake, olive-pale
       To   leeward, —
On the weather-side, black, spotted white with the wind :
" Good fortune departs, and disaster 's behind," —
Hark, the wind with its wants and its infinite wail !

ur fig-tree, that leaned for the saltness, has furled
       Her five fingers,
  n leaf like a hand opened wide to the world
       Where there lingers
No glint of the gold, Summer sent for her sake :
How the vines writhe in rows, each impaled on its stake !
My heart shrivels up, and my spirit shrinks curled.

Yet here are we two ; we have love, house enough,
       With the field there,
This house of four rooms, that field red and rough,
       Though it yield there,
For the rabbit that robs, scarce a blade or a bent ;
If a magpie alight now, it seems an event ;
And they both will be gone at November's rebuff.

But why must cold spread ? but wherefore bring change
       To the spirit,
God meant should mate His with an infinite range,
       And inherit
His power to put life in the darkness and cold ?
O, live and love worthily, bear and be bold !
Whom Summer made friends of, let Winter estrange !

AMONG THE ROCKS.

O GOOD, gigantic smile o' the brown old earth,
   This autumn morning! How he sets his bones
To bask i' the sun, and thrusts out knees and feet
For the ripple to run over in its mirth;
   Listening the while, where on the heap of stones
The white breast of the sea-lark twitters sweet.

That is the doctrine, simple, ancient, true;
   Such is life's trial, as old earth smiles and knows.
If you loved only what were worth your love,
Love were clear gain, and wholly well for you:
   Make the low nature better by your throes!
Give earth yourself, go up for gain above!

Cambridge : Printed by Welch, Bigelow, & Co.